Applying Linguistics in the Teaching of Reading and the Language Arts

The Charles E. Merrill
COMPREHENSIVE READING PROGRAM

Arthur Heilman
Consulting Editor

Applying
Linguistics in the
Teaching of
Reading and the
Language Arts

Catheryn Eisenhardt
Newark State College

80969

CHARLES E. MERRILL PUBLISHING COMPANY

A Bell & Howell Company   *Columbus, Ohio*

To teachers who encouraged me
To children who inspired me
To my family who sustained me
This book is dedicated . . .

Published by
Charles E. Merrill Publishing Company
A Bell & Howell Company
Columbus, Ohio 43216

International Standard Book Number: 0-675-09088-1

Library of Congress Catalog Card Number: 72-75764

1 2 3 4 5 6 7 8 9 10 — 76 75 74 73 72

PRINTED IN THE UNITED STATES OF AMERICA

Preface

In but a score of years there have been rumblings, shocks, and reverberations in the structure of the elementary school curriculum. Modern science, probing into vast outer space as well as into the minute atom, has deluged us not only with new and as yet unassimilated knowledge but with modifications of past beliefs. Until fairly recently a college student who wrote that the atom could be split could very conceivably have flunked the quiz. Likewise, an elementary school student writing about a trip to the moon could be dabbling in the realm of pure imagination.

Encouraged by government grants, institutes and scholarships, educators have translated the rapidly advancing knowledge of the disciplines into the curriculum plans of schools. Arithmetic has now become the *new math,* and science has moved from a token half hour in the week to an elaborate course of study designed to develop basic concepts in the early school years. The social sciences have been restructured and internationalized and include concepts from such disciplines as economics, anthropology and cultural geography—a far cry from the traditional history and geography. But what about the teaching of English? Yes, here too, there has been change brought about by research in language and linguistics. Some teachers feel these changes in English as tremors, while others experience them as shock. After all, while one can be objective about mathematics and science and even the social sciences, communication is a skill at the very core of existence—a set of values and habits, without which one feels uncomfortable, insecure and confused. That teachers intuitively rise to defend language against change is understandable even if not allowable. But "Believe it or not, we must be caught," and so this book has been written.

Its particular purpose is not to present a thorough description of the fields of linguistic inquiry. This has already been done by many authors, some of whom are listed in the bibliography. Rather, it is *to illustrate how the principles revealed by linguistic research can be translated into classroom practice.* In doing this, emphasis has been placed on:

1. A methodology which, in contrast to a dependence on the learner's passive acceptance of preconceived rules, offers opportunities for children to create knowledge based on their observations of language tested against their intuitive speech. They create their own sentences in terms of problems to be solved rather than break down sentences which have already been written. Their rewards are found in the realization that they possess both a power to manipulate sentences as they create language, as well as an appreciation for many styles of communication as they observe language.

2. A content which is structured to reveal the interrelationship of vocabulary, syntax, morphology and phonology as elements of meaning. This content can be found within the child who already knows his native tongue, the proof of which is found in his ability to speak and understand speech. It is the teacher who must know the names of the tools, but the naming in itself is unimportant. He must structure situations in such a way that children can discover for themselves what already "lies half asleep in the dawning of their knowledge."

With these purposes, the author, in testing the materials, has found them to be of particular help to students preparing to teach, to experienced teachers and reading specialists seeking methods to apply to the new content of linguistics, to teachers of children with non-standard dialects and to teachers of English as a second language. While the materials have been particularly significant in communities where language deprivation has created blocks to learning, the opportunity to observe language in a new way has challenged gifted groups.

This invitation to join those teachers and children who have extended their enthusiasm is issued with a special word of caution, for there are those who fear the climate of uncertainty and tentativeness which are a necessary part of the process of inquiry inherent in the materials. Linguistics is not for them. The author hopes that it is for *you.*

Catheryn Eisenhardt
March, 1972

Contents

Chapter One

*Then said a teacher, "Speak
to us of teaching." And he
said: No man can reveal aught
but that which already lies half
asleep in the drawing of your
knowledge."*
Kahlil Gibran—The Prophet*

The Content

The Language of Children
As a Basis for Language Study

At this very moment, as you read this, a cry is being heard around the world. It is the cry of newborn infants. In about three and one-half years these same infants, in whatever kind of home or in whatever part of the world they may reside, will become toddlers: toddlers who have already accomplished the most complex intellectual achievement of man —the acquisition of language. In probing for the explanations of this phenomena, researchers have revealed information that has made it possible to describe what a child does when he acquires language and in what sequence and under what conditions he does it. What has been found has already asserted a strong influence on teachers and curriculum builders. Hopefully when today's newborn appears at school he will find comfort and delight in his mother tongue rather than fear and frustration in graded language lessons.

The studies in language acquisition have been based on the linguistic word and sentence patterns identified by Charles Fries, † W. Nelson Francis and others. These findings will be summarized under three headings: 1. From Noise to Nouns; 2. From Me to Thee; 3. Variations in Complexity.

1. From Noise to Nouns

The first newborn cry which established the time of birth also marked the beginning of language. The fact that it is an involuntary

---

* Kahlil Gibran, *The Prophet*, p. 56. Copyright © 1923 by Alfred A. Knopf, Inc.
† See bibliography, pp. 131–33.

gush of air through the lungs aided by a good sharp slap on the buttocks in no way detracts from its message. It announces, *I am here.* As a result thousands of dollars will be spent for cards, telephone calls, knitting needles and footballs. From the moment of this first cry the course of language development in the normal child will correlate with physical development and follow a firmly fixed sequence. It will be modified by the environment only in terms of quality and speed of development but not in terms of the *order* of development. This will follow an unwavering course.

The birth cry, a noisy proof that the lungs are present and the system is *go,* is soon replaced by soft gurglings. These accidents of sound are produced by the muscles which cause the swallowing, sucking, gasping, hiccuping and crying movements. The changes that will occur in the anatomical and neuromuscular systems control the order in which his sounds will be produced. First are the short vowels heard in *bit, bat, bet,* etc., and the gasping and crying consonant [h]. Later, when he holds his head erect, he produces the nasal sounds. The eruption of the first teeth produces the labial sounds.

But does language depend only on maturation patterns? Is the emerging language of this sweet, soft newborn to be explained in such mechanistic terms? To do so would extol the wonders of the body as a machine, but would exclude the wonders of the body as a person. Language not only emerges as a spontaneous act as described, but also is dependent upon the emotional qualities of a supportive environment. The cuddling during feeding and the patting for the burp are all one vague but delightful sensation intermingling with these prelanguage sounds. The baby reaches out, touches the adult face, and explodes a gurgling "ahoo." The reward is equal to that given to the author of a best seller. Why shouldn't such effort be repeated? He plays with his vocal apparatus and becomes ecstatic over the discovery that the sounds were produced by him. To reassure himself he keeps repeating until he finally comes to the conclusion—"Yes, unbelievable as it may seem, it's me." ("It's I" is postponed for formal education.) The loving environment responds to this linguistic scientist by repeating a sound in the mother tongue that is equivalent to the child's sound. Thus the Oriental child will not have his [l] reinforced but instead will hear [r], accounting for such mispronunciations as "wrong" for "long" and "fright" for "flight" when he later learns English as a second language. The Spanish speaking child will not develop the short [i] but will develop long [e] accounting for "I leev here" instead of "I live here." In this way certain phonemes produced in vocal play are reinforced while others are discarded and fade away. The child's phonemes are now unique to his environment and are no longer global.

Then comes that glorious day that baby nonchalantly utters his first noun. At this point he goes beyond the communication level shared by all animals and enters the language level unique to humans. Just as the first cry communicates "I am here," the first noun proclaims, "I am." Language takes over and so does baby. He not only stands alone physically but also commands with single words all those that inhabit the earth—from puppy dogs who foil him to grandparents who spoil him. Who needs more than a single word when "Mama" can get him a cookie, a diaper or many things depending on the intonation and gestures accompanying the request. In response, the adult not only gives the cookie or changes the diaper but also expands the child's one word communication to a full sentence. "You want a cookie? Mommy will give her sweetie a cookie." Click click goes that little language computer. His English language phonemes are being ordered into words and sentences.

2. From Me to Thee

Impressive studies done in this decade reveal observations of how children develop the complexities of the English sentence in two years— from the tender age of one and one-half years to the risk-taking age of three and one-half. Before these findings were revealed it could be assumed that children produced sentences by imitation. That is, the child, after hearing repeated sentences made by the adult, would produce the model. This seemed like a logical explanation until the recordings of the speech of eighteen to twenty month old children revealed that they not only produce sentences that they have never heard before but also construct consistent patterns which do not have the features of adult speech. The few samples* that follow will sound familiar to the English-speaking adult who has spent even a short time with a talkative toddler.

two boot (boots)   Adam coat (Adam's coat)
No do that (Do not do that)   Baby cry (Baby is crying,
All gone cookie (The cookie   baby cried, will cry)
  is all gone)

It must be admitted that there is no evidence of imitation here, for no adult, even those using what is termed baby talk, would speak in such forms. The explanation offered for this stage of language learning is that the child does not imitate the adult but rather that the adult in a sense imitates the child. The first utterance is made by the child according to

---

* David McNeill "The Capacity for Language Acquisition," *The Volta Review* 68 (January, 1966) 17-32.

his established infant grammar. The adult repeats the intent of the child's speech in an expanded pattern supplying the inflections, word order and verb forms that were omitted. For example, "There Santa Claus" is repeated as 'Yes, there is Santa Claus." By hearing such expansions the child gradually makes adustments in syntax as he did earlier in phonology until finally the primitive, universal grammar is modified to become the grammar of his environment.

After about two years of singing and chanting words and sentence patterns, the tender three and one-half year old becomes of age in language. He enters the world of adult syntax with the power to use every part of speech, every inflection on nouns and verbs and every type of sentence found in adult speech. For example he would say (or understand) "I like my teacher" but would be confused by the utterance "Like my I teacher." English word order is already imbedded in the unconscious. He knows that "one dog" can become "two dogs" (syntactically and not biologically speaking), that "smile" can become "smiled" and "tall" can be "taller." On the other hand, he must tolerate the arbitrary, illogical and unpredictable adult who won't let him say "gooder" as he said "taller" or "two mans" as he said "two dogs."

3. Variations in Complexity

The child entering school will proceed on a language continuum from short kernel sentences to longer compound sentences, then to sentences that are made compact by the use of subordination. The extreme end of the continuum and the supreme goal of language learning is marked by the ability to produce a variety of patterns and to relate the selection of pattern to the style desired in the communication.

At this point there may seem to be a contradiction between what is described here and what is often observed by the teacher in the classroom. A distinction must be made between language *competence* and language *performance*. A child's competence reflects ability to understand word order and structures that make up complex sentences even though he cannot produce them in speaking, writing, or reading. The child's competence rests on his automatic and intuitive control. He just can't describe what he knows. There is often a big gap between the ability of competence and that of production, and the latter cannot proceed without the former. Because language performance is more obvious and measureable, it has been emphasized in the curriculum. The sensitive teacher with the knowledge of how language develops will relate language teaching to a *stage* rather than to an *age*. She will find each child's instructional level: that is, the point at which he feels comfortable in the use of language. Some six-year-olds can be at age two and one-half on the scale while others may be linguistically mature. Their needs are not reflected in a curriculum which splinters the description of langauge and then assigns fragments to each grade level. Language isn't learned this way.

What has been discussed here might be summarized as follows.

1. Children have an inborn predisposition to acquire language.
2. There exists an infant grammar revealed around the age of eighteen to twenty months.
3. The child tests his infant grammar against the presentation of adult models.
4. Without direction, the child follows a particular sequence of events suggesting that there is a hierarchy of difficulty. The order is:
   A. Phonology precedes all elements of language. Involuntary speech sounds are reinforced or discarded depending on the sounds of his environment.
   B. Single words which identify things in the environment are supplemented by gestures and intonation to express a sentence.
   C. Two words, then three words are put together in consistent patterns known as infant grammar.
   D. Word order is established.
   E. Function words are inserted.
   F. Inflectional and derivational endings emerge.
   G. The pronoun is introduced. Because the pronoun is so highly inflected and irregular in form, it is a difficult pattern to master.
   H. All basic patterns and all possible variations found in adult speech are present in the language competency of the preschooler.
   I. A difference between language competency and language performance is recognized.
   J. Sentence development follows the sequence from kernel to complex forms with the passive and subordinate transformations coming only when the child can think in the semantic complexities of those patterns.

Children, then, have several magically fruitful years to explore and to use language before coming to school. Yet, when they arrive, they will find teachers waiting to teach them English. *What will they learn? How will they learn it?* The answer will depend on the teacher and her commitment to a philosophy. The alternatives in language teaching? To say that there must be a choice between the traditional and linguistic descriptions is an oversimplification. Perhaps an eclectic approach—drawing on the principles of both systems—that suits both the children in the classroom and the teaching style of the teacher should be considered.

Who, then, are the linguists, what is linguistics and how can linguistic principles be applied in the classroom?

Linguists and Linguistics

The science of linguistics is not new. The period of the Renaissance with its trade, immigrations and inventions inspired a new interest in language study. Up to this time, Latin was considered the language of scholars, and since it was the scholars who wrote the textbooks it is understandable that they chose to use the prestige grammar of Latin as their model. Data from the inquiries into the historical and comparative aspects of language, however, supported a revolutionary new idea that was to give their work a new dimension. In essence it was that each language is unique and is to be described not in terms of some preconceived standard but solely in terms of what can be observed in the native texts of the language. A quick review of the history of English points out quite vividly the basis for this principle.

English is the result of several invasions that followed a relatively short visit of the Romans to the island of Britain. After the fall of the Roman Empire and the subsequent withdrawal of Caesar's legions from Britain, the Germanic tribes took over. These groups dominated Britain to such a degree that the earlier language was almost completely erased. In its place was a language that resembled the structure of modern German. There were grammatical genders that determined the case endings of nouns and their accompanying adjectives and, in addition, verbs had case and number. *Beowulf* is a classic example of this Early English period. The invasions of the Normans in 1066 marked an era that made such an impact on language that it was given a special name, Middle English. While William the Conqueror was primarily interested in political conquest, he brought with him the Latin-based Norman French language. In so doing he added French to the already existing German and Latin syntax and vocabularies. This mixture, together with the tendency to depend on word order rather than on inflectional endings to show relationships between words, paved the way for Modern English. Perhaps Chaucer, whose work is included in so many literature survey courses, is the best known writer of this period. A comparison of the works of these periods revealed that the influence of history gave English a syntax unique unto itself. Thus emerged the idea that each language is to be described solely in terms of its own pattern of sounds, forms, and meanings as they are revealed and objectively recorded, and not in terms of some preconceived standard (as: Graeco-Latin.).

This principle is the crux of the definition of linguistics: *Linguistics is a scientific inquiry into language which results in a body of verifiable facts.* Linguists, then, are scholars who use the scientific method of inquiry to understand and to describe the nature of language and how it functions. These scholars, like those in many fields, tend to specialize. Some, called *phonologists*, concentrate on the sound system of the language. Their studies revealed a regularity in word patterns. The *language historians* trace the changes that have occurred over a period of time. From such research came the second important principle—that change in language is inevitable and not haphazard. The *semanticists*, language sociologists, study meaning in terms of the setting of the communication rather than by the lexical meaning alone. The *dialectologists* have studied different speech communities. Their work has given new insights into the relationship of language to the history and culture of people living in different parts of a country. This awareness has fostered an attitude of appreciation and acceptance of differences. The *lexicographers* are the dictionary-makers. They are the recorders and not the makers of the language. Finally, the *grammarians* study the structure or the syntax of the language. They have developed a description of English that reveals a structure and form that has not previously been identified and, unlike earlier descriptions, *it can be taught at an early age.*

The work of the linguists might have remained the interest of a comparatively small group of scholars but for the fortunate link that was made between them and educators who recognized the possibilities for a new and vital approach to language. Through the concerted efforts of these two groups the subject matter of linguistics is being transformed into classroom action. The linguistically-oriented materials reflect a variety of interpretations of the research. Some linguistically-oriented materials have used the content but have ignored the fact that linguists have offered a *process* as well as content. A most important contribution of this new approach should be the development of habits of accurate observation of a language in process, together with an inquiring mind marked by curiosity. Students will thus learn not only the answers but how the answers are produced.

A Summary

Linguistics, then, is a body of facts about language gained through the process of scientific inquiry. These are the basic principles.

1. Each language has its own structure, and meaning is carried by means of this structure as well as through the vocabulary. The description of this structure can be taught at an early age.
2. There is more regularity in the phoneme-grapheme relationship than has previously been considered possible.

3. Language change is inevitable. This change should be considered a reflection of a dynamic culture rather than a sign of deterioration.
4. Dialects are part of a cultural heritage and one is not superior to another.
5. Usage is considered effective or ineffective in a given situation rather than correct or incorrect according to one arbitrarily imposed standard.

The Significance of Linguistics to the Classroom Teacher

Linguistics changes the image of the classroom teacher. First, the inquiry method places her in a role in which she guides children to discover and make generalizations about language. Second, the content has given her a new way of perceiving language and consequently a new way of structuring learning situations. What once seemed to be a string of facts which were spread through the textbook series from grade one to grade twelve becomes instead a structure which reveals the relationship of all the parts. The once divided elements of language are held together by the all embracing idea—how meaning is structured.

The smallest language structure is the phoneme, defined as the smallest *significant* speech sound. These sounds combine to form words. The fact that the phoneme-grapheme relationship isn't as haphazard as has been claimed opens a new approach to the teaching of word skills. For example, a large core of one-syllable words can be built on a basic consonant, vowel, consonant (C.V.C.) word pattern. This pattern can in turn be expanded, creating a tremendous corpus of regularly-patterned words. This opportunity to construct and find regular relationships replaces the memorization of word lists. The regularity and predictability of these patterns fosters a feeling of confidence in the approach not only to spelling but to reading as well.

Just as patterns are found in the word unit, they are found also in the sentence unit. An analysis of English sentences reduces them to basic patterns from which all complex sentences can be generated. For example: a *noun, verb* pattern could expand as follows:

Children play (N, V)
What kind of children? *Happy children.*
Where?   (at camp)
When?   (in the summer)

The expanded pattern thus becomes: In the summer, happy children play at camp.

Frequent opportunity in oral language to expand kernel sentences in this way and then to transform them into a variety of structures gives children an internalization or feel of the sentence. Meaning, now, becomes more than a definition of words, for words have no precise meaning until they are placed in a certain order in a sentence with the appropriate inflectional or derivational endings. These signals are in turn controlled by an intonational pattern signalled in writing by punctuation. For example, the difference of meaning between the utterances *What's that coming in the door?* and *What's that coming in? The door!* is a difference of intonation, an intuitive skill. This difference in meaning in the written form is a difference of punctuation, a learned skill.

Since the elements of word order, word form and intonation are already known to the young, native speaker, he becomes his own textbook. He is led to observe and analyze what he has done intuitively, to interpret his data in the framework of the above description of meaning, and then to come to some conclusions about his language. For the young child, the examples from which the generalizations are made are kept simple and within his experience. For the more mature student, the examples become more complex and sophisticated. The teacher evaluates a child's language production in terms of his development of syntactical patterns which reflect the long term goal of language instruction, i.e., the ability to construct and choose between a variety of patterns.

The teacher has a great responsibility to guide students to make choices in usage and to understand but not necessarily to reject patterns that differ from their own. The principle of appropriateness and effectiveness is taught with the standard forms. Recently a graduate student who was teaching sixth grade in an inner-city school became interested in this explanation of levels of speech in contrast to the traditional theory of *correct* and *incorrect*. Her class, she said, used the lowest and often the vulgar levels of usage. She found it awkward to impose the textbook structures which they held in scorn. Furthermore, in criticizing them, she criticized their families and friends. Since the new explanation seemed reasonable, she tried it.

Before the semester was over she arrived at her college class with this story. Every opportunity was used to tell them about different dialects and usage patterns of various communities and professions. Because her students were particularly interested in sports, she drew heavily on sports page vocabulary. While it was made clear that differences in language patterns and levels were interesting, it was also emphasized that they had the responsibility to learn the language appropriate to the classroom—standard English. Her big moment came, when, during oral reports, one of her most resistant boys rose, and with an emphasis produced by a waving fist, said to the student reciting: "Can dat low lebel stuff. Yer in are classroom now." These students knew about classification levels, and, what's more, they gained a new respect for themselves as well as for the teacher and what she represented. The teacher? She said she no longer felt so frustrated and was able to move them along toward the language goals.

As the teacher recognizes a variety of usage patterns, she must also recognize variations in dialect. Phonic generalizations which are based on standard English cannot always apply to the divergent pronunciation. For example, the generalization that the sound [oi] is spelled *oy* in *boy* and *oi* in *oil* cannot apply to a dialect that pronounces *oil* as *erl* (Brooklyn) or as *ol* (black area dialect). In such cases, no matter what the textbooks say, *oi* and *oy* do not represent the same sounds. Likewise, *swing* and *morning* cannot be taught as rhyming words in dialects that habitually pronounce *ing* as *in*. At one time, children were forced to make adjustments to the text or fail. In most cases they failed. Now, with the teacher's knowledge of how language works, she assumes part of the responsibility by making the adjustments, whether it be to a foreign language or to another dialect of her own.

Because the main purpose of this book is to explain the application of linguistic principles, the theory of the research is necessarily limited. For this aspect the reader is referred to the bibliography at the end of this book. New theories and materials will always be challenged and certainly should be, but at the same time teachers must also feel the obligation to study the findings that research in language has revealed.

It is the author's experience that these new facts about our language are forcing educators to restructure materials, and most of all to adopt new methods. Watching children discover that intonation controls meaning and that punctuation is a fascinating tool within their control rather than a page of rules imposed upon them; watching them approach spelling by searching for regular patterns and making appropriate generalizations rather than memorizing lists of words; watching them choose and discuss an effective sentence; watching them evaluate words or phrases in terms of social or regional dialects instead of filling in blanks that call for information foreign to the language that they hear and see about them; watching them become involved in such a way that they feel their own worth as they realize that they know something—all this is convincing evidence. Discovery replaces defeat or submission, and this seems to be an ingredient important to all learners.

A Summary

1. Linguistic research reveals a description of a grammar that can be taught early.
2. The description emphasizes a system of signals as well as the analysis of each one.
3. The subject matter of teaching materials is familiar to each child—his self-produced sentences. This is predicated on the realization that children have an intuitive control of language upon school entry.
4. The description of the sentence is in terms of both formal and informal situations so that the definition reflects the language environment of the child.
5. The methodology stimulates an attitude of inquiry and curiosity.

Suggestions for Further Study*

1. Scan the preface or introduction of a dictionary. Is it traditionally or linguistically oriented? What were your clues? If you find dictionaries with old copyright dates, compare them to current editions.

2. Read the section on *language history* in the preface of a dictionary. What facts support the principle of change in language?

3. Read *New Views on Grammar* in the *World Book Dictionary* (new edition) designed for children. What does this description mean to you as a teacher of English in terms of the content of your teaching?

4. In books printed before 1900 (go back as far as you can) find examples of language change in vocabulary, spelling, punctuation and syntax. Relate these findings to the principle of language change presented in this chapter.

5. React to the claim in this chapter that linguistic methodology gives the English teacher a new image.

6. The Society for Simplified Spelling recommended a revision toward simplified spelling in which the sound [s] as in *Sam* would be spelled with *s* and never with a *c* as in *city*. Also, the

---

* These suggestions may be studied in greater depth after the exercises in the handbook have been completed.

sound [z] would never be represented by *s* as in *dogs* but as *z*. Make just those two proposed changes in the following sentence: *Citizens with dogs and cats in cities deserve the seven cents tax.* How do you feel about the aim of the society? What counter-proposal results from linguistic research on word patterns?

7. What is meant by the sentence used in the text, "A child becomes his own textbook"?

8. How can the findings of research in language acquisition affect the methods and content of the English curriculum?

Chapter Two

The Sound

Intonation Described

The sound patterns of a language range from the single sound, the phoneme, which is similar to a note in music; to the largest sound, the intonation pattern, which is similar to the melody and rhythm in music. While intonation is found in all languages, it doesn't affect the meaning of the communication in quite the same way that it does in English. For example, one of our American Indian languages has an arbitrary pitch contour with high pitch on the stressed syllables and low pitch on the unstressed syllables of every two syllable word. It follows, then, that intonation in that language is mechanical and therefore does not influence the meaning. The role that intonation plays in an oriental language was described by a military friend who pointed out the confusion that could develop if the word *ban* were said with the wrong intonation. Five possible meanings depending on the pitch contour would be *to sell, table, desk, friend* or *sign.* A dramatic example can be found in Vietnamese in which the same word means *friend* and *shoot.* While the word is the same, the intonation is different. Just think of the possible consequences if one weren't acquainted with the tonal requirements.

In some languages, then, intonation is a mechanical feature having no bearing on meaning. In others, it is within the word, entirely changing the lexical meaning. In English, we will find that it influences a word or an entire sentence. For example, *"End* punctuation" said with the emphasis on the word *end* means something far different than the same

---

* William Shakespeare, *Hamlet,* act III, sc. 2, line 1.

sequence, "End *punctuation*" pronounced with the emphasis on the word *punctuation*. Likewise, the pause heard in "Teachers, do not complain." presents a different message than the same sequence said without the pause, "Teachers do not complain." Even a single word communication can be changed by the pitch pattern as in "No" (meaning, I won't do it) and "No?" (meaning, You won't do it?). It is important to note that in all the sequences described above only the intonation was changed; the words, word order and word forms remained the same.

The intonation patterns of English are described in terms of pitch, stress, and juncture.

Pitch

The feature of pitch refers to the rise and fall of the voice in speech. The non-technical term could be tone, the variations of which produce a melody. An example of this feature at work can be found in the sentence, *He's handsome*. This sentence said as a statement with the voice dropped at the end simply gives some lucky girl information about her blind date. Pronounced, instead, with a lift in the voice, a quality of surprise and delight is added. Or, if the receiver of the message wished to have the fact confirmed, she would simply pitch her voice in another way, turning the statement into a question, as, *He's handsome?*

Exercises assigned to students in which they are to identify sentences as declarative, interrogative, exclamatory or imperative seem to ignore this feature. The following sentence is typical of such an exercise: *The boys are at the station*. According to the teacher's manual, the sentence is declarative. Reading it in different contexts as described below should reveal other possibilities.

1. You are saying it in answer to the question, Where are the boys? *The boys are at the station.*
2. A friend just told you that the boys were at the station and you expected them to be at the airport. You question the information. *The boys are at the station?* (Note that the question form does not necessarily use inverted word order as in, *Are the boys at the station?*)
3. On hearing the information that the boys are at the station you are shocked because at this time they should be at the reading clinic. *The boys are at the station!*

Do you agree that the sentence in the first context would be declarative; in the second, interrogative; and in the third, exclamatory?

In the interrogative reading of the sentence, *The boys are at the station?*, a rise in voice signalled the question. Although textbooks persist in instructing children to read questions in this way the information is only partially true, as you shall see. What if, as you sit reading this, you suddenly started to sing aloud. Since this behavior is strange to you, you stand in surprise at yourself and say: *What hit me?* (down). Again, suppose someone said to you, *Where are you going?* (down again) Now, not being quite sure of what they said, you answer, *Where am I going?* (This time the voice went up.) Exploration of the question intonation patterns will reveal that the voice goes up or down depending on the type of question. Children, fortunately, use the right pattern intuitively and shouldn't be blocked with misinformation.

The English Language Institute devised a system to mark the pitch pattern as follows: A line just under the letters indicates pitch two; a line well under the letters indicates pitch one (the lowest) a line just over the letters, pitch three: and the line well over the letters, pitch four (the highest).

For example,

Mary is planning to go to college

The pitch contour is declarative. But someone is not quite sure that they heard you and says

Mary is planning to go to college

The slight rise of pitch signals a question. This news seems to be very surprising so another person says

Mary is planning to go to college

The higher rise in pitch signals the exclamation.

Stress

Another feature of intonation is stress. The non-technical term might be accent or loudness. This should not be confused with pitch which is higher or lower while stress is loud or soft. Examples of the stress feature are found in the following sequences:

Would you feel more successful if you had baked a *short* cake or if you had baked a short *cake?*

Have you ever seen a match *box?* No, I didn't say a *match* box, I said a match *box.*

These examples may seem amusing but the power of stress can be observed in serious situations including a court of law. There is a story of a lawyer who was called to defend a young mother on a charge of murdering her baby. She was about to be found guilty on the testimony of a nurse who reported the mother as saying: *How can anyone get rid of a baby?* When the nurse repeated it in cross examination, however, her emphasis was on the word *can. How CAN anyone get rid of a baby?* The nurse also agreed that the mother was fondling the child when she said it. Not only was the placement of stress important but also the context in which it was said.

Now shift from courtroom to classroom while a book is being discussed.

Teacher	Boys and girls, you have just read the story, Jack the *Giant* Killer. What did Jack do in the story?
Student	He killed giants.
Teacher	How would you describe Jack?
Student	He was strong. He could kill giants. . . .

Now listen to this version.

Teacher	Boys and girls, you have just read the story, Jack the Giant *Killer.* What did Jack do?
Student	He killed. He was a killer.
Teacher	How would you describe Jack?
Student	He was big. He was a giant. . . .

What a difference that one shift in stress made. With very little effort a *giant* killer was recognized as being very different from a giant *killer.* Are you beginning to understand the influence that this feature of language can have on reading comprehension?

Juncture

The third feature of intonation is juncture or pause. Juncture refers to the various kinds of division points in the flow of speech. Sometimes the pause is slight as found within a word like *anything—any thing.* A longer pause is found between grammatical parts of a sentence as observed in:

This class thinks its teacher is the best in the school.

Or

This class/thinks its teacher/is the best in the school.

Or

This class thinks. Its teacher is the best in the school.

Shakespeare's awareness of this element of speech is reflected in the following passage from *Othello,* Act III, sc. 1.

Cassio   Dost thou hear, my honest friend?
Clown   No, I hear not your honest friend. I hear you.

The longest pause marks the end of a sentence or is the silence between two sentences. This can be heard in the third version of the examples above. Note the longer pause after the word *thinks*. When the voice fades away in this kind of completion the end of a sentence is intuitively felt. The emerging definitions of a sentence do include this principle of intonation. The pause certainly is not just something that refreshes. It controls.

Three features of intonation have been identified: stress, pitch and juncture. That the intonation pattern superimposes a meaning on the lexical meaning in a sentence, that intonation is used effortlessly by a native speaker of the language and that the ability to use it started so early in the development of language that the native speaker is unaware of its presence has been explained.

What is the significance of this information to the classroom teacher? Out of what seems to be disorder, a system has been discovered. The use of intonation is not haphazard. While it may be intuitive in its use, it is no longer necessary to depend on the child's intuition to recognize it or on the teacher's intuition in teaching it. It has a system with its specific vocabulary; precise description can replace the phrase *with expression*. Too, a teacher with the knowledge of this element is better able to give emphasis to the *interplay between the speech that is internalized in the child and the print which is to be learned*. This becomes particularly valuable to a child who reads *Oh, no grandmother, said Bunny* for *Oh, no, grandmother, said Bunny*. The next example is from an older, but no more advanced reader, who read *In Alabama, where she had lived before, her family moved to Chicago* for the text version, *In Alabama, where she had lived before her family moved to Chicago*.

The power of intonation is not confined to the literal level of comprehension but extends to the fine nuances of interpretation. The study of the relationship of sound and style to the interpretation of a communication has been traditionally postponed to advanced literature classes but now such observations are being made as early as kindergarten. Listen in on a kindergarten dramatization of *Pussy Cat, Pussy Cat*. As the children discussed one presentation, it was noted that "Mike talked nasty." Mike came to his own defense by saying "She asked me nasty." After a second try done in dulcet tones, Mike responded in a peaceful, charming way. The teacher was quick to take the opportunity to point out the importance of the principle *the way you say it*.

A similar experience occurred in a fifth grade which was observed during an oral reading session. A student read a story about a boy who was so interested in art that he played hookey so that he might spend the day painting. After a long dialogue with an artist who pointed out the value of an education, the story ended with the boy saying, *I must go to school.* I then asked the reader how he thought the boy felt about his decision. He responded by giving a long explanation which I interrupted to explain that I wanted to know how the boy felt by hearing the way the final line was said. No words were to be added. Nothing was to be changed. The class caught on to the idea and presented several versions. One child said it with an intonation that conveyed the idea that he was really convinced. Another child's version suggested that he was going but very reluctantly. Another was accepting but not convinced. The interpretation, they found, was completely in the choice of intonation pattern made by each reader. All the versions were in contrast to the first reading which was done as though the words had appeared in a list.

Now, listen to some seventh graders applying this principle to the reading of Richard Hovey's *Sea Gypsy.* The first reading was done with the typical stress patterns noted here.

> I am *fev*ered with the sunset.
> I am *fret*ful of the bay,
> For the *wander*lust is on me
> And my *soul* is in Cathay.

After this first reading, other intonation patterns were tried. They resulted in the following interpretations.

1. Stress the words: *fevered, fretful, wander, soul* and *Cathay.* This, they said, sounded very whining.
2. Stress the word: *I, I, me, my.* This sounded boastful.
3. Stress the words: *sunset, bay, wander, soul, Cathay.* This was wistful.
4. Stress the words: *am, am, is, is.* This was positive, forceful and arrogant.

These students were discovering many possible interpretations and had the right to choose the one that best suited them. Their real learning was in the discovery of possible differences rather than in the acceptance of one and only one correct meaning.

Intonation and Punctuation

After working with elements of intonation in this way, students very quickly discover that there is a relationship between their voice signals and the marks of punctuation. Rather than memorize preset rules and then try to choose the rule that applies to the communication, he asks himself what he wants the reader to do with his voice when he reads and then he inserts the mark that will give the proper signal. The marks of punctuation, then, are considered a shorthand code for telling the reader what to do with his voice. Test this by listening to what your voice does in response to punctuation signals used in these sets of sentences.

The Comma and Stress

1. In which sentence is the questioner a polite cannibal?

   Shall I eat teacher?   *Shall I eat, teacher?*

2. In which sentence did Pam die?

   Pam, the kitten died.   *Pam, the kitten, died.*

3. Which sentence is uncomplimentary?

   Now look stupid.   *Now look, stupid.*

4. In which sentence is the dress and not necessarily the child beautiful?

   A beautiful child's dress.   *A beautiful, child's dress.*

The End Punctuation and Pitch

As the comma signalled the juncture in the above sets of sentences, the marks of end punctuation have a relationship to the pitch levels as demonstrated in these examples.

   You wouldn't dare? (Wouldn't you really?)

   You wouldn't dare! (I defy you.)

   Why is it long?

   Why? Is it long?

The students who can read such passages "trippingly on the tongue" must certainly feel the power of intonation and its effect on punctuation. Testing their own sentences against their reading them aloud in this way has done much to prevent run-on and choppy sentences. This suggests a different system of theme correction for the teacher. Instead of making the usual specific corrections, he marks all incorrect passages *RA* which means "read aloud." The student who does this invariably discovers his own mistake and can make his own correction. The teacher need not reserve the use of *RA* for incorrect sequences but can also use it to mark passages that seem particularly effective.

Conclusions

With this background of information in mind, the materials that appear in the handbook section have been designed to help the student discover the connotative power of intonation. Since this discovery can only be made in situations that require speaking and listening, the methods stress oral experiences. Following each experience, opportunity is provided to analyze what was done and to arrive at the following generalizations about language from the data.

1. Intonation controls meaning.
2. There is a relationship between intonation in speech and punctuation in writing.
3. Intonation not only controls the literal meaning of a sentence but also affects the tone or style.

Suggestions for Further Study*

1. Read the section on *punctuation* found in the preface of a recent edition of a dictionary. In what way does the information support the idea that intonation and punctuation are related?

2. In the same or similar sources, find evidence that intonation is a factor in the modern definition of a sentence.

3. Find examples in prose and poetry that illustrate how various intonation patterns can change the meaning or interpretation of the writing.

4. How can you relate intonation to reading comprehension? Give examples.

5. Discuss in terms of the information given in this chapter regarding children's intuitive control of language: The first task of language instruction should be to give children an opportunity to make generalizations about the language that they know on the intuitive level.

6. Find jokes, riddles or anecdotes that use the technique of shifting stress patterns as a basis for the humor.

---

* These suggestions may be studied in greater depth after the exercises in the handbook have been completed.

7. As you read newspapers, be alert to headlines that make good examples for the effect of the shift of stress on meaning.

8. If you know a person who is learning English as a second language, discuss the difficulties they might have with the intonation patterns of American speech. How do they learn to use this power which is natural to the native speaker? How could you explain a rule for certain elements of intonation?

Chapter Three

There are nine and sixty
ways of constructing tribal
lays and every single one of
them is right.
Kipling—"In the Neolithic Age"

The Structure

The Sentence Defined

What is a sentence? The search for the answer reaches back to 1 B.C. when Dionysius of Thrax defined it as *Suppositum est illud, do quo fit sermo, appositum est illud quod dicitur supposito.* A free translation reveals that a sentence has the properties of a subject, a predicate and a complete thought. In 1894, John Reis published his study of the sentence and the result was the listing of one hundred and forty definitions, all of which referred to the same three elements. These definitions, as the examination of language texts would reveal, continued through the centuries.

Teachers seem to agree that the concept of a sentence, when described in these abstract terms, is very difficult to teach young children, and in fact, the not so young as well. Then too, the definition does not make allowances for such structures as the preposition at the end of the sentence or the words *and* or *but* at the beginning. In the meantime, the young reader encounters them in the literature and mass media that surrounds him. Life English just doesn't seem to be the same as textbook English when he reads such delightful sequences as: *Can you imagine? A fluffy, puffy kitten* or *But not Eeyore!*

The definition not only fails to describe sentences as they are found in actual use but also is inconsistent as a base for sentence testing. For example, in a sequence like *The birds are singing* there is no difficulty. There is a subject noun, a verb, and a complete thought. Yet the same words are present in the sequence *the singing birds,* which isn't considered a sentence. A fourth grader made this comment about the structure, "It has a noun and a verb and it's about birds and they're singing. It must be a complete thought." This inquiring student could have been helped with an explanation of word order which is not present, however, in the definition.

Consider next the example *I have*. It contains a subject noun and the verb but is it a complete thought? This is difficult to determine out of context but it is out of context that sentences to be identified are presented in textbooks. The example *I have a headache* is complete in every element of the sentence test but, if *I have* is already a sentence, one might ask, why isn't *I have a headache* a run-on sentence? This may sound foolish to the reader who is trained to think in terms of the traditional definition, but admissably it is a logical deduction for the child struggling with grammar.

Try testing the sentence *I heard her*. This is certainly complete with noun, verb and complete thought. But what if in saying this sentence the reader failed to lower the pitch in his voice as he would naturally have done in a statement signalled by a period? In this case, there would have been a suspended feeling which is represented in writing with a dash, as in *I heard her—*. The reader waits for information to come, as for example, *I heard her (sing)*. Both sequences, *I heard her* and *I heard her—* had the elements of the sentence; but only the first, read with the lowering of the voice at the end, was a sentence. The second was not. What made the difference? The intonation. This element of intonation has become an important base for the linguistic definition. An examination of current texts, dictionaries and language studies will support this. Rather than the intonational base, some linguists describe the sentence in terms of the syntax, that is, in terms of word order and word form. For example, *Jack the hill went up* would not be accepted because of its word order any more than *a buggy baby* would be accepted as a substitute for *a baby buggy*. The forms *s* and *'s*, for example, express facts of plurality and possession when attached to words. Without these signals the facts would have to be expressed in separate sentences. For example, the sentence *The boy's dog did tricks* would become three sentences: *The dog did trick. Dog belong to boy. More than one trick.*

Working with the elements of intonation, word order and word form, linguists have been able to reduce the great variety of possible English sentences to certain basic patterns which are described in the handbook section of this book. With the basic patterns identified and described in this way, the process of expansion is put to work to develop a variety of English sentences. This is done by adding modification structures to the basic pattern as follows: *The boy threw the ball* is a basic N^1 V N^2 pattern. A certain quality and identification is given to the noun *boy* by adding such words as *tall, handsome, teen-age*. The noun can be further modified with the addition of the phrase, *who goes to Briarwood School.* Likewise, the object noun *ball* could be modified with the word, *winning.* The verb, too, can be expanded by adding information that tells how, *with excitement;* when, *last night;* where, *in the basket.* The result of these units clustering the nouns and the verbs is: *Last night, the tall, handsome, teen-age boy, who goes to Briarwood School, threw the winning ball into the basket with excitement.*

Rather than start with the unknown on the abstract level of definition, then, the student starts with the sentence model which he manipulates through certain sequenced developmental stages outlined below.

The Structure of Meaning

Level I.   Getting the feel of the sentence by the process of
    1. Intonation
    2. Use of basic patterns manipulated by
      a. substitution
      b. expansion

Level II.   Gaining power in constructing and reading complex sentences by the process of
    1. Compounding
    2. Coordination
    3. Subordination

Level III.   Making choices between a variety of patterns by the process of
    1. Recognizing the relationship between
      a. syntax and sound
      b. syntax and style
    2. Recognizing the relationship between the intonational pattern of the sentence and the interpretation

The student who has many opportunities to manipulate these structures orally and in writing quickly perceives the relationship of the modification units as he meets them on the printed page. In short, there is a transfer from the description of language and how it works to the processes of composing and reading.

The sentence, then, is not perceived as an abstraction but rather as a communication constructed through finely related devices that pattern in an intriguing variety of ways. The ingredients are the lexicon (the words); the syntax (the word order and word form); and the intonation (stress, juncture and pitch). These signals and how they pattern and show relationship to each other determine the sentence. Methods for developing these skills will be presented in detail in the Handbook, Section Two.

A Summary

The linguistic definition of the sentence as described seems to have these advantages:

1. There is a transfer from the definition of the sentence to the processes of composing and reading.

2. Since the elements of the definition are already imbedded in the child's language, the concept of the sentence can be taught in the early school years.

3. Instead of rules, the child's intuitive language competency forms the base for observation and analysis.

4. The elements, because they are already present in the child's language, can be taught as a system rather than as a series of abstractions stretching out over the school years.

5. The definition includes sentences that the child finds in print and not just the formal sentences of the textbook.

Suggestions for Further Study

1. Collect from anywhere and everywhere—basal readers, textbooks, professional literature, children's literature, children's writings:
   a. Sentences that begin with *and* or *but*. Show them in context by including the preceding sentence of the text.
   b. Sentences that end with a preposition.
   c. Sentences that, according to the traditional rule, are fragments but are effective in the context.

---

* These suggestions may be studied in greater depth after the exercises in Sections Two and Three of the handbook have been completed.

On the basis of the above observations come to some conclusions regarding the traditional definition of a sentence.

2. What is meant by "the transfer from the intuitive control of language to the ability to analyze and describe language"? Describe how this concept can influence your methodology in language teaching.

3. Discuss the values of manipulating a variety of patterns from the basic sentence as described in the text and handbook.

4. Reading comprehension exercises have emphasised vocabulary and content but have ignored the structural signals of meaning. React to this statement.

5. Read the following carefully so you will be able to answer the questions that follow.

The kragerier multiness grabulated the wogg
of the klug bremuously.

Can you name the parts of speech? How did you identify the nouns without knowing the meaning of the words? How did you identify the other parts of speech? Discuss in terms of traditional vs. linguistic descriptions of word classification.

6. Discuss the following quotation. "We have taught the signs (e.g.: plural endings, possessive forms, punctuation marks) but not the system."

Applying Linguistics in the Classroom

The materials in this handbook are designed to apply the linguistic principles previously described. It is divided into three main sections. Section One, Working with Intonation, provides experiences in listening to, saying and analyzing the speech patterns of American English. There are five units in this section, the first four developing the concept of intonation and the fifth relating the marks of punctuation to each of the elements of intonation observed. Section Two, Constructing and Expanding Sentences, provides experiences in composing and manipulating sentences based on linguistic sentence patterns. The materials are arranged from simple expansions to more complex sequences using subordination and compounding. This follows the continuum of language as found in the language development of the child.

While each unit contains a series of experiences that develop a specific element under study, it is not necessary to complete every example before proceeding to the next unit. In fact, after a concept has been discovered it is advisable to move into another area and then to return to known materials for reinforcement and broader application. Note that the statement of purpose that precedes each lesson is written *for the teacher* to guide him in structuring the learning situation. If it were revealed to the children before the lesson, *the whole element of discovery would be removed.* Hopefully, the concept expressed in the purpose will be elicited from the students as a generalization. While possible answers are provided in brackets for the various experiences in these two sections, they are included as materials against which the reader can check his own constructions. Section Three, A Reference for Teachers, provides a handy reference for teachers who may not be familiar with linguistics. Eight sentence patterns and parts of speech as described by linguists are presented and basic linguistic terms are defined. Included is *The Story of Punctuation* which provides excellent background material for the study of punctuation in Section One.

Recognizing that no handbook can provide a complete set of materials, it is hoped that the experiences described here will serve to trigger fresh and creative ideas appropriate to the classrooms in which they are used. Children working in these ways should feel both the delight of observing and analyzing language, and the power of manipulating it.

Working with Intonation

This section not only introduces the concept that intonation controls meaning, but also provides oral language opportunities for the learner to hear and to listen to the patterns and sounds of language. In so doing he internalizes the feel of the sentence, which is important to his writing and reading skills. Because intonation is intuitive to the native speaker of English, it offers a convenient point of reference for the more difficult skills of language study.

UNIT 1.
GENERAL EXPERIENCES IN LISTENING
TO INTONATION

Teacher's Purpose. To discover that meaning is communicated not only by words, or by the order in which words are placed in a sentence, but also by the intonation of speech. The elements of intonation are stress, juncture and pitch, which are represented to some extent in writing by punctuation.

Experience

Teacher's Purpose. To discover that the intonation of an utterance affects the meaning.

Directions

The only word that you are able to say is *oh.* Direct class to say word with the expression (intonation) appropriate to each situation as described. As you do this, ask these questions: Did each *oh* as it was said have a different meaning? How can we describe what caused the differences?

Situations

1. You have just opened a birthday gift.
2. You have suddenly turned over on your ankle.
3. The principal has just announced that school will be dismissed early.
4. A wet puppy jumped up on you.
5. You are watching a magician pulling a rabbit out of a hat.

In the discussion, encourage the labeling of the emotions. For example, in Situation 1, a child could say that he was *happy and surprised*. In Situation 4, they might be led to express the difference between *displeased surprise* and *happy surprise*. When several situations have been dramatized, begin to build the generalization stated in the purpose set for these experiences.

In the following variations, use the same procedure described above.

Variation

Use the word *please* instead of *oh*.

Situations

1. You want someone to move over in line.
2. You want your friend to go to the movies with you but he has already seen the film.
3. Someone is annoying you by tapping a pencil on the desk.

Variation

These are similar to the above exercise but done in dialogue rather than in solo form. You will need a partner to do this.

> *Mother*   Where have you been?
> *Boy*   Playing baseball.

Situations.   (These can be written on separate cards and given to participants.)

1. Act out the dialogue as though the mother were just casually interested and the boy played a miserable game.
2. Act out the dialogue as though the mother were just casually interested and the boy had a real winning streak.
3. Act out the dialogue as though the mother were really annoyed and the boy was tired of hearing her ask questions.

> *Mary*   Did you get a new brother or a new sister?
> *Sue*   A new brother.

Situations

1. Act out the dialogue as though Sue had three sisters and wanted a brother.
2. Act out the dialogue as though Sue had three pesty brothers and wanted a sister.

Variation

Read the sentence *I'm going to the movies* with the expression appropriate to each situation described.

Situations

1. You are happy and telling everyone.
2. You're inquiring to see if it's true.
3. Your mother doesn't want you to go but you insist.

Variation

Pantomime situations appropriate for the sentences given below. Speak only the sentence but pantomime the situation leading up to the spoken statement.

I gave her BABY food.   I gave her baby FOOD.
I gave her DOG biscuits.   I gave her dog BISCUITS.

Discuss: Were the pantomimed situations different in each contrasting sentence? What caused the difference?

The previous exercises were planned to sensitize the student to the power of intonation in a very general way. Now each of the elements of intonation with its concise vocabulary will be discovered and described.

UNIT 2.
EXPERIENCES IN LISTENING TO THE ELEMENT OF STRESS

Teacher's Purpose.   To discover that meaning is controlled by a change in the position of stress, which is one element of intonation.

Experience 1

Directions

Read the sentence in a way that would be natural to the situation that will be described to you. Remember that *you cannot change the words, add or omit words, or change the order of the words.* (Note:

The scientific process requires that just one change be made at a time.)
Say the sentence:

I sit here.

1. Emphasize where you sit. (I sit *here.*)
2. Emphasize that you sit and do not stand. (I *sit* here.)
3. Emphasize who sits. (*I* sit here.)

In discussing this generalization with children, elicit a more specific term than intonation. Accept any word that expresses the idea of placing more emphasis on a certain word. The technical word to work toward is *stress.*

Experience 2

Directions

Read each phrase below placing stress as marked. Draw pictures that would illustrate the meaning of each phrase. Compare the illustrations. Are they different? Explain in terms of the purpose.

high school	high *school*	*house* fly	house *fly*
bank roll	bank *roll*	kitchen *sink*	*kitchen* sink

Let a collection of the above illustrations form an amusing review as well as an opportunity to develop a flexibility in speech as the various captions are read.

Variation

Instead of illustrating, put some of the above or similar phrases in dialogue form as follows. Remember that these are suggestions, so give the children opportunity to compose their own.

Which would you prefer: A short *cut* or a *short* cut?   I'd prefer a
(insert preference) because (state reason).
Did you ever see a board *walk*?   No, but I've seen a *board* walk.
Joan said we could see her new kitchen *sink*.   Don't you mean her
kitchen sink?

Experience 3

Directions

I'm going to name a particular person. Listen carefully and then tell us how you think the person would be dressed.

A bride's *maid*

Any answer is acceptable that brings out the idea of a servant and not a member of a wedding. Now do the same for this person.

A *bride's* maid

The answer to this should certainly be in contrast to the first, as this time, the maid was a member of the wedding.

Experience 4

Directions

The answer to the following riddles would be given away if the stress were improperly placed. Can you explain what you must do to read these riddles properly?

1. Does your watch tell *time*?   (Yes)
   Does your watch *tell* time?   (No, it never tells time. I have
       to look at it.)
2. How many hairs in a bunny's *tail*?   (Hundreds)
   How many hairs *in* a bunny's tail? (None. They're on the outside.)

Variation

Bring in books of riddles to read to the class. Point out specifically how the shift in stress can effect the understanding of the riddle. Note that this would be a very difficult exercise for students learning English. Perhaps some of the more linguistically mature students could test these patterns and make up a rule for the placement of stress that would help a non-native speaker.

Experience 5

Directions

Newspaper headlines are printed in telegraphic form and can be very misleading if read with the improper stress patterns. Choose the stress pattern you wish to use in the following headlines. Write an opening paragraph appropriate for the stress pattern you chose.

Vatican Phones to Get New Look

Draft card burners

Village Well Blasted by Arabs

Examples of responses from young students follow:

Vatican Phones to Get New Look—According to a Vatican bulletin, the phones there are to be modernized etc.

Vatican *Phones* to Get New Look—A call was received from the Vatican requesting that the United States look at the decision to etc.

Draft *Card* Burners—It was the opinion of one group that card burners should be drafted etc.

Draft Card Burners—Students who did not submit were referred to as draft card burners.

Variation

Listen to the following headlines as they are read. Be ready to answer the questions that follow.
1. Air Hearings at Rutgers. Are the air hearings at Rutgers or will they air the hearings at Rutgers?
2. Missing Prisoner Hides in Jail. Did a missing prisoner hide in jail or are the missing prisoner hides in jail?

Variation

Here are some signs for you to read. What a confusing world this would be if we didn't have control over our intonation!
1. SIGNAL AHEAD (There's a signal ahead or Send a signal ahead?)
2. CROSSWALK AHEAD (Is the walk cross?)
3. STRETCH SOCKS (Will you stretch the socks?)

The examples presented thus far have demonstrated how stress can effect the literal meaning of a communication. It should be noted, however, that meaning can go deeper than surface facts and that a mood or attitude can be expressed by the intonation pattern. The following experiences are planned to develop this concept.

Experience 6

Directions

Read the verse below. Underline with colored chalk the words that you choose to emphasize. After you read it as marked, underline a different set of words. Read the versions as marked by different members of the class. Listen for the change in tone. What can you say about the relationship between intonation and interpretation?

If all the world was apple pie
And all the sea was ink
And all the trees were bread and cheese
What would we have for drink?

The following version were offered in an elementary classroom:

If all the world was apple pie
And all the sea was ink
And all the trees were bread and cheese
What would we have for drink?

There's a kind of impatience. The person saying this is standing with his hands on his hips and his head held high so he can look down his nose.

If *all* the world was apple pie
And *all* the sea was ink
And all the trees were bread and cheese
What would we have for drink?

There's a real concern or worry. The person is looking at you with a worried frown. His voice is soft. His shoulders stoop over a little.

Variation

Divide groups with each group presenting its version in choral speech. The reaction of groups reacting to various versions of one selection rather than to varied selections is interesting and original.

Don't stop with these few examples. The real value of this experience comes when students make their own selections and can explain the different moods or interpretations that resulted from the change in stress patterns.

UNIT 3.
EXPERIENCES IN LISTENING TO THE ELEMENT OF JUNCTURE

The power of stress has been demonstrated. This unit will present experiences that demonstrate the power of juncture or pause. As you work with this unit, it is suggested that you link the lessons with appropriate punctuation exercises found in Unit 5.

Teacher's Purpose. To understand that when the voice pauses and immediately continues on a slightly higher pitch, meaning is changed.

This feature of intonation will be called juncture or pause. Juncture can occur within a word, between words or groups of words, and between sentences.

Experience 1

Teacher's Purpose.   To discover that meaning is controlled by the position of the juncture in a word.

Directions

Use the following phrases in a sentence showing the contrast in meaning as the position of the juncture in the italicized word is shifted.

Example:
along	Get *along,* little doggie
a long	Get *a long* little doggie
Nineties	*Nine T's*
across	*a cross*
I scream	*ice cream*
useless	*use less*

Variation

Dramatize the above sequences in such a way that the effect of the shift in juncture position will be demonstrated. These are examples of some classroom experiences.

Jen	I scream when I see the ad.
Nan	What ad?
Jen	The ice cream ad.
Ken	Did you say the soap powder was useless?
Mike	No, I said that I use less.

Experience 2

Teacher's purpose.   To discover that meaning is controlled by the position of the juncture between words.

Directions

Read both versions aloud. Listen carefully and be ready to answer the questions:

1. In which of the following sequences is the child beautiful? In which is the dress beautiful?

   A beautiful child's dress.   (the child)

   A beautiful/child's dress.   (the dress)

2. In which of the following is the light bright blue? In which is the blue light bright?

   A bright blue light.   (the color blue is bright)

   A bright/blue light   (the blue light is bright)

Variation

Sequences like those above may be dramatized so that phrases can be set in a natural setting. Examples of some classroom response to this assignment follow:

1. A fresh/peach sundae   A fresh peach/ sundae

Setting: A favorite local ice cream store.

Characters: Customer and soda clerk.

Customer	I'd like a fresh peach/sundae.
Clerk	O.K. (He opens up a can of peaches.)
Customer	I asked for a fresh peach/sundae.
Clerk	This is a fresh/peach sundae.
Customer	It's not a fresh peach/sundae. I saw you opening the can.
Clerk	It is a fresh/peach sundae. I just made it.

2. A half/baked chicken   A half baked/chicken

Setting: A diner.

Characters: Customer, waitress and short order cook.

Customer	I'd like a half/baked chicken.
Waitress	(calling out the order to the chef) One order for half baked/chicken.
Chef	(calling back) Half baked/chicken coming up.
Waitress	(serves the plate to customer who becomes enraged)
Customer	I don't want this. I ordered a half/baked chicken.
Waitress	This is a half baked/chicken.
Customer	But I didn't ask for a half baked/chicken. I asked for a half/baked chicken.
Waitress	Oh! You want a half/baked chicken. Not a half baked/ chicken.
Customer	Right!
Waitress	(sighs with relief and leaves)

Experience 3

Teacher's Purpose.   To discover that meaning is controlled by the placement of the juncture in a series of items.

Directions

Listen to the following sentence as I *read* it to you.
We had chocolate ice cream cake and candy.
How many items were on the menu? (chocolate ice cream cake/ candy)
Note: Remind students that they are to listen to the number of items as you have said it and not to the possible number of items if it were phrased differently. Now change the menu by changing the position of the pauses. No other changes can be made. Do not change the word order or add or omit words. This is important. Say as many versions as you can. After you do this, check with the following menus discovered by one class.

chocolate ice cream cake/ and candy
chocolate/ ice/ cream cake/ and candy
chocolate ice/ cream/ cake/ and candy
chocolate ice cream/ cake/ and candy
chocolate ice/ cream cake/ and candy
chocolate/ ice cream/ cake/ and candy

Read the different groupings until you discover the idea that it is the position of the juncture that makes the big difference in the menus (as well as in the calories!).

Variation

While this experience is fresh in your mind, try these sentences that are similar in structure. This sequence can be dramatized with a shopper and storekeeper who must produce the desired items. One class presented a hilarious sequence in which the shopper phoned in the request and went to everyone including the president of the company to get the order straightened out.
1. I bought vanilla chocolate and strawberry ice cream cakes and milk.
2. She bought butter milk chocolate cream cheese coffee cake jelly rolls and bread.

Variation

Listen to these sentences. Listen for the pause and then answer the question.
1. How many items did Betsy throw on the floor?

Betsy threw the dish towel and sponge on the floor.
Betsy threw the dish/ towel and sponge on the floor.
2. What do you prefer?
   I prefer pizza/ pie/ cake and cookies.
   I prefer pizza pie/ cake and cookies.
3. How many will be there? What are their names?
   Mary Ann/ Bill and Joan will be there.
   Mary/ Ann/ Bill and Joan will be there.
4. How many hobbies do you have?
   My hobbies are camping/ hunting/ cats/ and reading.
   My hobbies are camping/ hunting cats/ and reading.

Experience 4

Teacher's Purpose. To discover that the junctures in the structures traditionally taught as direct address and appositives affect meaning.

Directions

Act out the following dialogue. (Note: Put large name tags on each participant as this will make the shift in meaning clear as the lesson develops).

Situation. Miss Smith is sitting at her desk when the principal enters. The principal is followed by a new teacher.

Principal (to Miss Smith): Miss Smith/the new teacher has arrived.

Direct class to repeat the sentence as it was stated by the principal. Repeat the sequence as much as necessary to identify the pause heard between *Miss Smith* and the remainder of the sentence.

Now try the contrast version known traditionally as the appositive.

Situation. The class is waiting to meet the new teacher. The principal enters with the new teacher whose name is *Miss Smith*. Note: Direct children to name the characters and to decide on the name cards needed. Probe to reach the conclusion that the teacher being introduced will have two cards: *Miss Smith* and *the new teacher*.

Principal (to class): Miss Smith/ the new teacher/has arrived.

Does this second pause change the meaning? Repeat the readings of both sentences until the class gains a flexibility in switching from one form to the other.

Variation

The following sentences are similar in structure to those above. Read the contrast forms to listen to the differences. Direct class to make up dialogues to suit each version. Just deciding on the characters and their names probes into the comprehension of the sentence. For example, in Sentence 1, the speaker and Dan (a boy) would be necessary while in the contrast version a speaker, the person being spoken to and Dan (a dog) would be necessary. Of course, if you don't want the dead dog present as evidence, that can be done, without affecting the comprehension!

Examples:

Dan/ our dog is dead.	Dan/our dog /is dead.
Steve/ an artist painted these models.	Steve/ an artist/ painted these models.
Now my friends listen when I talk.	Now/ my friends/ listen when I talk.
Give the ball to her son.	Give the ball to her/ son.
Shall I wait for her mother?	Shall I wait for her/ mother?

The following is an example of what one class did with the sentence

Please phone Tom and say we can't come.

Situation:	Mr. Blake is reading the newspaper when Mrs. Blake comes in excitedly.
Characters:	Mr. Blake, Mrs. Blake and Tom (who never really appears).
Mrs. Blake	Oh dear! There go all our plans. We have a message that my brother is arriving from Europe and we are to meet his plane.
Mr. Blake	But we have a date to play bridge with Tom and his wife.
Mrs. Blake	We'll just have to cancel it. Please phone Tom and say we can't come.

(Mr. Blake goes to phone. Fade out.)

Contrast version: Please phone/ Tom/ and say we can't come.

Situation:	Nancy and Tom have just finished dinner. Tom is helping Nancy with the baby.
Characters:	Nancy and Tom.
Tom	Junior doesn't seem to be too happy tonight.
Nancy	He must be getting another tooth. He's so irritable.
Tom	I believe he's a little feverish, too. Do you think we should go to Jim's house tonight?

Nancy   Oh, no. I wouldn't leave Junior with a baby sitter. Please phone/ Tom/ and say we can't come.

Variation

I will say something to you and you are to give me an appropriate answer.

You're pretty sick.

Elicit any possible reactions that would make appropriate dialogue.

Now react to this version of the sentence. Would you say the same things?

You're pretty/sick.

Repeat the exercise with these sentences:

He bought Ronnie a horse.	He bought Ronnie/ a horse.
When do we feed the baby mother?	When do we feed the baby/ mother?
Students do not complain about homework.	Students/ do not complain about homework.

Experience 5

Teacher's Purpose. To discover that the junctures in the structures traditionally taught as parenthetical units, restrictive clauses and non-restrictive clauses, affect meaning.

Directions

Note that the main part of the structure is read on one pitch while the parenthetical unit is read on another, and that the parenthetical unit is set apart from the main sentence by the use of juncture. Read the following sentences and listen to the intonation pattern. Mark the main sentence with one colored chalk and the parenthetical unit with another. For keener listening direct one group of the class to read the main sentence while another group reads the parenthetical unit. Repeat this as often as necessary to feel the rhythm and sound pattern of the sentence.

Example: Group 1.   A mouse
                    Group 2.   the tiniest white one
                    Group 1.   broke loose in the classroom.
Tom/ who won the race/ will get the prize.
In division/ for instance/ you must know your number facts.
The girls/ who didn't finish their homework/ will stay after school.

Note that the last sentence in the above group could be said without the pause as: *The girls who didn't finish their homework will stay after school.* Now the meaning is changed.

Read the first version and then the second to hear the contrast. Exaggerate a little if necessary. Direct the class to decide who was staying after school in the first (all the girls). Who would stay after school in the second? (the girls who didn't finish their homework).
Practice with these contrast sentences.

1. The boys who study hard will get A's. (not all the boys?)
   The boys/ who study hard/ will get A's.
2. The girls who are pretty will be in the contest. (not all the girls?)
   The girls/ who are pretty/ will be in the contest. (so many pretty girls)

UNIT 4.
EXPERIENCES IN LISTENING TO THE ELEMENT OF PITCH

Two elements of intonation—stress and juncture—have been introduced. This section will present the third element, pitch. Pitch is the raising or lowering of the voice and can be compared to melody in music. It should not be confused with loud and soft, which is stress. For example, read the following sentence as a question. *I can see you?* You signalled this as a question by raising your voice to a higher tone at the end. This is pitch. Now read the same sentence as a statement and at the same time emphasize the word *you. I can see YOU.* This time the pitch went down and the stress was louder.

Teacher's Purpose.   To discover that there is a relationship between the pitch used in speech and the meaning of a sentence.

Experience 1

Teacher's Purpose.   To discover that the change in pitch at the end of a sentence can change the meaning.

Directions

Write the following sentence on the board without punctuation. Direct a group, or the whole class to read the sentence aloud in such a way that it would be appropriate to the situation to be described.

The lights went out.

Situation 1.   You've come to school without your homework. I've asked the reason and you say: (read sentence).

Situation 2.   I don't quite believe you and say: (read sentence).

Situation 3.   You're walking through a dark, damp, gloomy deserted hallway. suddenly you hear a voice that sounds like crying. Then you say: (read sentence).

Discussion.   Elicit purpose. Note that there could be a realization that unpunctuated sentences out of context could be declarative, exclamatory, interrogative or imperative depending on the intonation given by the reader.

Variation

Continue the purpose and format of the above experience but this time direct the class to make up situations that would elicit different pitch patterns. Try it with the sentences that follow and then write your own.

1. He had his hair cut today
2. He's out
3. The clock stopped at midnight
4. A mouse
5. Try it

Variation

Put some of the above situations in short dialogue form and then act them out. Here are some examples from other classrooms.

Situation 1.   Elizabeth wants to go swimming and is telephoning her mother for permission. We listen in on the scene just after Elizabeth has asked for this permission.

Characters:	Elizabeth; her friend, who is standing by; her mother at the other end of the line.
The communication:	*No*

Mother	No.
Elizabeth	No? (disappointed)
Mother	No! (emphatically) (Both hang up)
Elizabeth's friend	No? (listening in)
Elizabeth	No. (in disgust)

Situation 2.   Tom is visiting his friend in the infirmary.
Characters: Tom and Bud.

Tom   How do you feel?
Bud   O.K.
Tom   O.K.?

Situation 3.   Scott wants to back out of a driveway but because tall
bushes obstruct his view, he is depending on Bob's signals.
Characters: Bob and Scott.

Bob   O.K. Go.
Scott   Go? (In the meantime a speeding car approaches.)
Bob   Stop!
Scott   Stop? (crash! bang!)
Bob   Oh! (in excitement)
Scott   Oh. (groaningly)

Experience 2

Teacher's Purpose.   To discover that the pitch is not always upward at
the end of an interrogative sentence. (Note that this is opposite to what
is traditionally taught.)

Directions

Write the sentence
Where do you think you're going?
on the board. Direct class to read the question with a pitch pattern
appropriate to the situation you will describe. Listen carefully in each
instance for up or down pitch.

Situation 1.   You've just heard that your brother is shipping out and
you ask: *Where do you think you're going?* (down at the end?)

Contrast   Now emphasize the word *Where* when you read the question.
(down at end?)

Situation 2.   You are speeding and an officer stops you and asks:
Where do you think YOU'RE going? (down?)

Variation

For added testing, try these dialogues.
1. Who won the game? (down)
   John.

John won the game? (up)
2. Why isn't Roy playing? (down)
Did you say, Why isn't Roy playing? (up)

UNIT 5.
PUNCTUATION AND INTONATION

Students working with the oral experiences described in previous sections probably have already discovered the relationship between intonation and punctuation. Instead of thinking of punctuation marks as symbols representing long lists of rules, they perceive them as graphic representations of features of speech—pitch, stress, and juncture. In other words, the punctuation mark is equivalent to a whole sentence in that it says to the reader: Do this with your voice here to keep the meaning that I (the writer) intended. Conversely, the writer says: I must place the marks here so that I can signal the reader what I mean. The period, question mark and exclamation mark signal pitch, while the comma signals the pause within a sentence. The colon, semi-colon and dash represent pauses longer than those signalled by the comma. The contextual meaning is usually enough to signal points of emphasis or stress, but sometimes there is a need to make them clearer; then underlining or italics is used. Note that punctuation marks used in such sequences as addresses, letter headings, dates, etc., are not to be included in this concept, as these are arbitrary forms to be learned.

The Comma

Experience 1

Teacher's Purpose.   To relate the use of the comma to the pause or juncture used in speech.

Directions

Repeat the sentence introduced in Unit 3 above:
We had chocolate ice cream cake and candy.
(Any sentence of similar construction could be used.) Ask: How could you make the menu clear if you couldn't talk to a friend but had to write to him?
Do not accept the answer, *use commas.* Remind them that punctuation hasn't been invented yet. Elicit as many solutions as possible, such as putting in list form or placing lines or dashes between. Emphasize that many things might have been tried long ago to make communica-

tions clear until someone had the idea of punctuation marks. (See: *Story of Punctuation* at end of this Handbook.)

Variation

Review again the sentences in Unit 3 (Juncture). Usé them for dictation, directing the students to write and punctuate what they hear. Compare. Discuss.

Variation

This can be done the same way as the dictation exercise above, but this time proper names are used. It is this kind of sentence that so often confuses students when they try to follow the rules. Let the pause be a guide.
1. John, was Mary here on Sunday?
2. Have you seen Tom lately, Ben?
   Have you, Ben, seen Tom lately?
3. Which story should I write about Ann?
   Which story should I write about, Ann?
4. It's my turn to wash Sally.
   It's my turn to wash, Sally.

When students have difficulty in hearing the differences in these sequences, introduce more oral experiences like those in previous units. Dramatizations of single sentences are effective.

Variation

Read the following ads from newspapers and magazines. Note how the meaning was changed as the pause signaled by the comma was changed.
1. Duncan Hines Cake, so moist, friends will ask for your recipe.
   Duncan Hines Cake, so moist friends will ask for your recipe. (Hm. Such friends)
3. Ford's ride is amazingly quiet. (So you like your car.)
   Ford's ride is, amazingly, quiet. (You didn't expect it?)
3. No matter how you wash or dry them, Cannon towels are guaranteed. (Good)
   No matter how you wash or dry, them Cannon towels are guaranteed. (Usage)
Follow through: Find your own examples in mass media. Read both ways by playing flexible or shifting commas.

Variation

Follow directions as in above exercises but find sentences in themes and texts. Practice on these.

She bought red, white and blue plaid, and flowered materials.
She bought red, white and blue, plaid, and flowered materials.
Was Lincoln, the sixteenth president, born in a log cabin?
Was Lincoln the sixteenth president born in a log cabin?

Exercises like those already presented develop the principle that the comma divides the sentence into meaningful units. Because textbooks are not in agreement about certain rules regarding the use of the comma, these differences will be investigated here. Some texts claim that in the *series pattern* the comma must be used before the final *and* in a sentence. Others say that it need not be used, while others say it doesn't make any difference. The following experiences are designed to investigate these differences.

Experience 2

Teacher's Purpose. To discover that the use of the comma before the final *and* in a series is not always an arbitrary decision but depends on whether it is needed to make the meaning clear.

Directions

Read the following sets of sentences as punctuated and answer the questions that follow each set.
1.   The teacher gave us pencils, paper, and art supplies.
Was the meaning clear? (Yes) Read the sentence punctuated without the final comma.
     The teacher gave us pencils, paper and art supplies.
Was the meaning clear? (Yes) Were the number of items changed? Did it make any difference whether or not you used the final comma? (No)
2.   Joan, Mary, and Alice are going to the movies
How many were going to the movies? Was the meaning clear? (Yes) Read it without the final comma.
     Joan, Mary and Alice are going to the movies.
How many were going to the movies this time? Act out both sentences. Did you see how quickly the second version became the structure of direct address? Did it make any difference whether or not you used the final comma? (Yes)
3.   They had blue, green, and red and gold balloons.
How many varieties? What were the colors? Read it without the final comma.
     They had blue, green and red and gold balloons.

How many varieties? What were the colors? Was the meaning changed? (Yes)   Did it make any difference whether or not you used the final comma? (Yes.)

4.   At the school fair were the teachers and fifty students who
               ate the hamburgers and the principal.
How could you save the principal with the use of a comma? Did it make any difference whether or not you used the final comma? (Yes)

In your discussion, elicit facts that would lead to the concept expressed in the purpose and emphasize how the word groupings are controlled in speech.

Experience 3

Teacher's Purpose.   To discover that the pause that is represented by the comma in a series is used not only to separate sentences into meaningful parts but also to give emphasis to the parts that follow the pause. While this does not affect the basic meaning, it does affect meaning in the sense that it sets a tone or style.

Directions

Read the sentences as punctuated.
               He threw the dish, towel and sponge.
               He threw the dish, towel, and sponge.
Was there a difference in meaning? (No) Was there a difference in style? (Yes) Elicit observations that bring out such statements as *slower, last item seems more important,* etc. Test your observation on sentences you find in texts or in Unit 3 of this handbook.

Variation

Read these sentences with and without the final comma. Which reading is more apt to elicit the remark in the parenthesis?
1. She ate pizza, chocolate pie and banana split. (A banana split too!)
2. He caught a perch, a flounder and six large bass. (Incredible! Bass is so scarce.)
3. She is beautiful, charming, and intelligent. (Not intelligent, too!)
4. She took English, French and Greek. (Greek is so difficult.)

Experience 4

Teacher's Purpose.   To discover that the use of the comma after an opening phrase or clause is used not only to separate the sentence into meaningful parts but to control the style or tone of the sentence.

Directions

Read the sentence aloud.

When the bell rang the teacher called the roll.

Was the pause needed to make the meaning clear? (Yes) Ask this same question as you read the following sentences. In each case, listen to what your voice does.

1. As the teacher lectured the children became more restless.
2. When we drove through North Carolina we saw the Great Smokies.
3. Because it was raining we went to the movies.
4. Suddenly it happened.
5. Obviously you didn't pass.
6. In the winter time passes slowly.
7. When leaving Ann was sad.
8. If you had ice cream sandwiches will not appeal to you.
9. Hoping for the best we took our tests.
10. Every Friday our teacher tells a story.

Now consider just those sentences in which the pause (and therefore the comma) was *not* necessary to control meaning (sentences 2, 3, 4, 5, 9, 10). Read them with and without the pause. If the pause did not control the literal meaning, what effect did it have on the sentence? Elicit remarks that develop the concept in the teacher's purpose. In doing this, dramatize the sentence and observe the kind of person or situation that would require the slower reading signalled by the comma and the kind that would not require the pause.

The Semicolon and Dash

Both the semicolon and dash represent pause in speech but they differ from the comma in that the pause is a bit stronger or more emphatic. On the other hand, the pause is not as final as that signalled by the period. The ability to make choices is best developed by listening first to the way the message is naturally communicated in speech and then transferring the sound to writing.

Because the structure is used by more mature students, little space is given to developing it here. The following examples should suffice in directing the teacher who has followed the materials provided for the use of the comma. Reading the alternate versions of sentences according to the punctuation and listening to the voice intonations that result should be convincing evidence that punctuation should be heard as well as seen.

Read and Listen

1. I wish to thank the faculty, the students and our honored guests.
   I wish to thank the faculty—the students—and our honored guests. (profound?)

2. Miss Penn, the most beloved teacher in the school, will retire.
   Miss Penn—the most beloved teacher in the school—will retire.
3. We discovered to our surprise that the team didn't win.
   We discovered, to our surprise, that the team didn't win.
   We discovered—to our surprise—that the team didn't win.
4. The bell rang. School was over for another year.
   The bell rang; school was over for another year.
5. He had a good reason for leaving the hikers. His feet were aching.
   He had a good reason for leaving the hikers; his feet were aching.
6. It really wasn't a very good game, yet it had its exciting moments.
   It really wasn't a very good game; yet it had its exciting moments.
   It really wasn't a very good game. Yet, it had its exciting moments.

End Punctuation

Experience

Teacher's Purpose.   To relate the pitch level of speech to the period, exclamation mark, and question mark used at the end of a sentence.

Directions

Refer to Unit 4 (Pitch). Direct one group of students in the class to read a particular pitch pattern while the remaining students write the sentence with the punctuation as they heard it. Repeat with alternate patterns.

Variation

The pitch that changes the meaning: Direct three members of the class to act out the following dialogue while the class listens to the different intonation given to the word *pink.*

Situation:	The scene opens at a store where Jean is buying a birthday gift for Roy. She chooses a pink shirt which Roy is not going to like.
Characters:	Jean, the clerk, and Roy.
Jean	(pointing to the merchandise on the shelf.)
Clerk	*Pink?* (not quite sure which shirt she is pointing to.)
Jean	*Pink.*
	The shirt is wrapped and given to Jean who leaves to meet Roy. Meets Roy in scene 2. Roy opens the package.
Roy	*Pink!*

How was the line punctuated? Act out the scene again but this time Roy will like the color *pink*. Was it said in the same way? Describe the difference. How would it be represented in punctuation? Punctuate the word *pink* as used throughout the script.

Variation

The following paragraphs give choices in the end punctuation of the key line. Decide on the meaning you wish to convey, say it aloud and decide on the punctuation. Discuss with the group the difference this choice made on the interpretation of the story.

1. The night was cold and damp. Scott had been walking aimlessly down the street. He had no place to go for he had run away from home. Suddenly there was a flash of lightning and a white figure could be seen through the trees. It was enough to make Scott tremble. Did he go home (?) (!)

2. Ellen walked jauntily out of eye doctor's office feeling like a new person. Now she wouldn't need to wear those heavy, old, ugly glasses. As she approached the door she felt a stab of pain in her eye. It was a cinder. She dashed inside, and, standing beside the sink, she removed the new contact lens. Suddenly, it happened. She stared dumb with disbelief and watched helplessly. It went down the drain (.) (?) (!)

Variation

Writing—Reader's Choice: Write your own paragraph leaving the key line for the reader to punctuate. Discuss as above. Some sentences to start with are:

I can't look at him   You're losing weight   Please

Variation

Find sentences in literature or text books that could be read with different pitch patterns. Ask: What happened to the meaning? What is the effect of proper use of punctuation signals on reading comprehension?

Quotation Marks

Experience 1

Listening to direct and indirect quotation patterns relating to quotation marks.

Teacher's Purpose. To discover that the direct and indirect quotation are expressed in speech by certain intonation patterns and that the word *that* traditionally taught as a signal for the indirect quotation is not always used in actual practice.

Directions

Dramatize the sets of sentences below. Listen to what the voice does. Decide on what characters are needed. How does meaning change?

1. Johnny said that his mother is going on the picnic.
   (Who's going? Who's speaking? Were there any internal pauses?)
   Johnny said his mother is going on the picnic.
   (If the meaning has not changed in these two sequences, can the word *that* be considered a consistent signal for direct address?)
   "Johnny," said his mother, "is going on the picnic."
   (Listen for voice pauses between quotation and rest of sentence.)
2. The teacher said that I'm good in English.
   The teacher said I'm good in English.
   The teacher said, "I'm good in English."
   (Note the meaning and intonational difference between the second and last version. Who does *I* refer to in each version?)
3. He said that I'm a good boy.
   He said I'm a good boy.
   He said, "I'm a good boy."
   (Ask the same questions that you asked in (2) above.)
4. She said, "I will go home."
   She said that she would go home.
   She said she would go home.
   (Which is the direct quotation? Are the last two sentences different or the same in meaning?)
5. Tweedledum said, "Tweedledee will break my nice new rattle."
   Tweedledum," said Tweedledee, "will break my nice new rattle."
   (Who will break the rattle? Is it the same in both versions? Elicit purpose.)

Variation

Refer to books of jokes and riddles. Rewrite the anecdotes in direct form. See the example below. Act out each version.

I met Jim and he asked me how I would get into a haunted house if the windows and doors were locked. I said I couldn't guess so he told me that I should use a skeleton key.

Jim   How would you get into a haunted house if the doors and windows were locked?

Friend   I can't guess.
Jim   You should use a skeleton key.

In discussing the ways of identifying the direct quotation, emphasize the difference that the intonation of speech made in each version.

Experience 2

Teacher's Purpose. To develop a sensitivity to the rhythm and sound of the direct and indirect quotation structures.

Directions

Instead of using words, place patterns of dashes on the board (see below). Direct the class to beat out the dashes. After they do this, direct them to chant the dashes as demonstrated in the examples below. After they get a feeling of the pattern, ask them to insert words that would fit the rhythm.

1. ____ ____, " ____ __ ____."
   da   da,   " da   d   da."
   She   said,   "Here   I   come."

2. "____ __ ____," ____ ____.
   " da   d   da ,"   da   da .
   "Here I come," she said.

3. ____ ____ ____ ____ __ ____.
   da   da   da   da   d   da .
   She said that she would come.

4. "____" ____ ____, "__ __ ____ __ ____."
   " da ,"   da   da , "d   d   da   d   da ."
   "Yes, said Jane, "I will come with you.

Continue this experience with original frames constructed by the students. In doing this, elicit as many sentences as you can that fit into the frames.

Variation

Use already constructed patterns from the exercise above but change the end punctuation of the quotation to elicit different messages. For example

Are you her friend? !
Close the door. ? !
I can't do it. ! ?
You use more than that. ? !

Variation

Write the following sentence groups with dashes as done above.

1. Mary said, "No, I can't go."
   "No, I can't go," said Mary.
   "No," Mary said, "I can't go."
2. "Tom," cried Dan, "catch the ball."
   "Tom cried, "Dan, catch the ball."

A Review

Experience

Teacher's Purpose. To relate all the marks of punctuation to the intonation signals in speech.

Directions

Listen carefully to the following sentences as they are read. It will be important to hear the different intonation patterns. Indicate the difference that you hear by using the proper punctuation marks as you write each sentence.

1. What's that coming in the door?
   What's that coming in? The door?
   What's that coming in? The door!

2. She too eagerly awaits.
   She, too, eagerly awaits.

3. Everyone I know has a secret ambition.
   Everyone, I know, has a secret ambition.

4. Don't forget it.
   Don't. Forget it.

5. Why must we do it?
   Why? Must we do it?
   Why must we? Do it!

Variation

Writing with flexible punctuation: Choose a version of a sentence set like those given above. Write a paragraph appropriate to the punctuation you chose. Read it to the class and direct them to punctuate the key sentence as you planned it. Following is an example of an exercise done in one class. Incidentally, they taped several of their products and in this way were able to hear their own voices.

A few days ago my friend, Joan, asked her friend, Bonnie, if she would come to our house the next day. Bonnie answered that she would like to but that she had a detention. Joan looked amazed because Bonnie was getting a detention every day. She turned to her friend and said "Why? Don't you ever shut up?"

(Contrast version.) Mary and Marion were good friends. Mary was the silent type and Marion was the kind of girl who had a large vocabulary and used it a lot. When they were half-way home one day, Marion's incessant non-stop chatter got on Mary's nerves so she turned and snapped at her friend, "Why don't you ever shut up?"

A Summary

1. Punctuation marks in writing represent the intonation signals of speech.
2. Choice of punctuation depends not so much on a particular rule as on a sensitivity to stress, pitch and juncture as they occur in speech together with a knowledge of the marks that represent these elements.
3. Punctuation practices as found in print vary, but in most cases the form represents the intent of the author.
4. Punctuation not only controls the literal meaning of a passage but the secondary interpretation or style.

Constructing and Expanding Sentences

This section on sentence construction and expansion is based on the assumption that language is already internalized in the child who is able to compose most of the basic sentence patterns of English as well as many of the expansions long before he arrives at school. He does this intuitively, however, without the ability to describe what he has done. This power of description need not be postponed until the child is able to cope with abstract terminology. It can be developed as soon as he begins school instruction by starting with sentence models* which he expands and then explains. In this natural setting of his own language environment, he can supply the information that is called for and then describe what he has *done in terms of the function of the supplied information.* The process is one of construction rather than dissection, shifting the purpose of language teaching and learning from the analysis of already composed sentences to the construction of one's own. Repeated oral and written exercises such as these give the child the feel for a sentence and for the added units as they function in the expansion. In turn, the ability to create in this way transfers to comprehension in reading as he becomes accustomed to units of meaning and how they relate to each other.

UNIT 1.
USING SUBSTITUTION

Teacher's Purpose.   To discover that
1. There is a basic sentence structure that does not change when new

---

* See description in Section Three of this handbook, pp. 96-102. Chapter Three, p. 25, outlines the continuum of development.

words are substituted in a pattern. The substituted word will have a different *meaning* but not a different *function* in the sentence. This is an important exercise to develop the concept of *nounness* and *verbness* in the young student before grammatical definitions are introduced.

2. Words that can be changed to plural form can be classified as nouns (words that name people, objects or things, or the words in this list).

3. Words that can be changed to past or future tense can be classified as verbs (words that tell what the person or thing is doing or the words in this list).

4. When the subject noun changes in number, the form of the verb also changes.

This link between the noun and the main verb is at the core of the standard English sentence.

Note: While grammatical terminology is used in this unit, the concepts can be developed without it. In working with the less linguistically mature student, simply refer to the *function intended* rather than to the name of the structure. This is suggested in the parentheses above.

Experience 1

Teacher's Purpose.   To discover that one noun can be substituted for another but (a) the sentence pattern remains the same, (b) its function in the pattern does not change.

Directions

Make a list of words that could substitute for the underlined word in the sentence: The boy is running (teacher, dog, water, etc.). In the sentence, the word boy tells us who is running. What word tells you who is running in your sentence? These words that you substituted have a special job (or function) in the sentence. Did that function change when you substituted your words? (No) Did the sentence pattern change? (No) Explain exactly what happened (See purpose).

Experience 2

Teacher's Purpose.   To discover that one verb (the word in this slot or place) can be substituted for another but the sentence pattern remains the same. When one verb is substituted for another its function in the sentence does not change.

Directions

Make a list of words that could substitute for the italicized word in the following sentence: The boy *is running* (is playing, plays, does jump, could laugh, etc.). In the sentence, *is running* tells us what the boy is doing. What words tell you what the boy is doing in your sentence? These words have a special job or function in the sentence. Did this function change when you substituted new words? Did the sentence pattern change? Could the words that were substituted for *is running* be put in the noun place? (other slot?) Could the words that were substituted for nouns be put in the verb place? (this place or other slot?) Explain (see purpose).

Note: In working with children keep a chart or chalkboard list of the substituted words. These can be used in subsequent lessons as a resource list for (1) sentence writing practice; (2) to put into categories according to function. Some teachers have had success by printing nouns on one color paper and verbs on another. This is later extended to other parts of speech. After these sentences are constructed by shifting the cards into a wide variety of possibilities, they can be copied in *a sentence book*.

Make small *sets* of word cards to be manipulated at student's desks.

Linguists test sentences by setting up *sentence frames* in which they substitute words that function in the same way. A frame for a noun would be: The _____ smiled. Or The _____ saw the _____ on the _____. A frame for a verb would be: The baby _____. The baby _____ here. He _____ her.

Experience 3

Teacher's Purpose. To discover that when the noun (words in this slot) changes to plural form, the form of the verb (words in this slot) also changes.

Directions

In the sentence below could you express the idea that there is more than one person performing the action without actually saying the words "There is more than one person"?

The boy runs (boys run.)   The teacher jumps (teachers jump).

Note: Both the pluralization of the nouns and the change made in the verb forms are made easily and naturally by the speaker of standard

English. In fact, it is done so naturally that one may well ask why it is necessary to construct such lessons. *First,* the experience offers opportunity to verbalize exactly what one does to structure a sentence. *Second,* the oral experiences help the student gain a feel of the rhythm of the sentence. *Third,* the simple manipulations form the base for the more complex techniques that will follow. These experiences are particularly significant to those who speak another language or dialect that does not include this noun-verb linkage in their grammars. This idea is developed in detail in the last chapter of this book, *When English is a Second Language.*

As children make these substitutions, it will soon become evident that all nouns do not form plurals by simply adding the letter *s.* This is a matter of knowing irregular patterns, however, and does not affect the basic principle being taught.

In discussion elicit discovery that two changes are made when singular nouns are made plural. (1) The form of the noun changes. (2) The form of the verb *also* changes.

Experience 4

Teacher's Purpose.   To discover that the idea of time can be expressed by changing the form of the verb.

Directions

What changes would you have to make in the sentence if the word *yesterday* was added to the sentence below?

(Yesterday,) The boy jumps. (jumped) (had jumped) (was jumping)

Note: When working with children, be careful to use regular verbs in these early lessons.

Variation

Continue to make a list of sentences. The word lists developed in earlier lessons can be used.

1. Substitute the past tense of the verb for the present.
2. Substitute the plural form of the noun with the past tense of the verb. Note that the tense change is in the auxiliary in forms like *were jumping.*
3. Substitute a word or group of words that express time for the word *yesterday* (*Last week, This morning, Before I came to school*).

Experience 5

Teacher's Purpose. To discover that the idea of future time can be expressed by adding an auxiliary to the verb.

Directions

Listed below are two sentences that you studied before.

The boy laughs.   Yesterday, the boy laughed.

If instead of the word *yesterday,* the word *tomorrow* was used as:

Tomorrow, the boy laughed.

What change would you have to make? Did you change the form of the verb? (No, you added the auxiliary, *will,* to perform this function.) Continue with children's sentences in this pattern.

Variation

Construct sentences that use:

1. Other future verb forms such as *may laugh, can laugh, will be laughing, is going to laugh,*
2. Other words or groups of words in place of *tomorrow,* e.g., *next week, eventually.*

Probe your sentences to discover that the words or phrases like *tomorrow* and *after school* can be omitted from the sentence but that the structural signal in the auxiliary cannot be omitted. Is this also true of time words used in past tense sentences? Test it.

Variation

Repeat the above exercises in the following sentence patterns:

1. The teacher dismissed the class.
2. The dog is faithful.

The exercises thus far have applied only to kernel sentences. The process of substitution, however, may be applied to any unit of an expanded sentence and offers an excellent method for developing variety and style in writing. These exercises will be referred to again in a later section when the reader will participate in substituting for other parts of speech and in manipulating a variety of patterns.

UNIT 2.
USING WORD ORDER

Word order is another basic principle in the construction of an English sentence. It is considered the most important device in English grammar by which meaning is controlled, and takes the place of inflectional endings, the grammatical device used in many other languages. The following exercises are designed to demonstrate this.

Experience 1

Teacher's Purpose. To discover that meaning is controlled by the position in which words are placed in the sentence.

Directions

Use the five words presented to make a sentence. Use each word just once but use every word.

teacher   the   children   scolded   the

What sentence do you have? The teacher scolded the children. The children scolded the teacher.

Does the meaning differ in the two sentences? Was the meaning changed by using different words? (No) By changing the form of the words? (No) Were any words added or omitted to change the meaning? (No) What exactly was done to change the meaning? (See purpose.) Incidentally, a young German student visiting one of our classes would see nothing wrong with the sentence, *Have you the book read?* Can you explain why?

Variation

Save the people mentioned in the following sentences by changing the position of the underlined words.

The lobster ate the teacher.
The ball hit the boy.
The bear bit the man.
The elephant sat on the lady.

Variation

Write your own *Save the people* sentences.

Construct a principle of sentence word order that you discovered by experimenting in this way.

Experience 2

Teacher's Purpose. To discover that adjectives (words that describe) must be placed before the noun they modify.

Directions

Add the word *fat* to the sentence below. Place the word in any position you wish as long as it makes sense.

The girl read the book.

The fat girl read the book.   The girl read the fat book.

How was the meaning of the two sentences changed? Construct a principle of word order that you discovered by experimenting with sentences in this way.

Variation

Apply the same procedure as used above with the following sentences.

The man painted the school. (insert *old*)

The boy used the pencil. (insert *dull*)

The teacher saw the principal. (insert *angry*)

The girl sang a song. (insert *pretty*)

In working with children encourage them to illustrate each set of sentences. Illustrations will clearly point out the big difference in the meaning of the two possible word arrangements. Encourage free discussion of the reasons why illustrations do or do not agree with the sentence. For example, in the sentence, *The girl sang a song,* one fourth grader showed both a *pretty girl* and a *pretty song.* When his classmates challenged him, he insisted that the song *had* to be pretty because the word was there but the girl could be pretty in your imagination. Who won is not so important as the fact that these children were sharpening their comprehension of sentences.

Experience 3

Teacher's Purpose. To discover that meaning is changed when the adjective is placed after the noun rather than before the noun it modifies.

Directions

Write the word *window* and the word *cleaner* on two separate cards. Close your eyes and pick up one word at a time. Write the words in the order in which you picked them up. Do this until two word order patterns are revealed.

Window cleaner   Cleaner window

Does the meaning differ in the two sequences? Explain. Was the meaning changed by using different words? Were any words added or omitted? What exactly was done that caused the change in meaning? (See purpose.) To reinforce this concept continue working with the following phrases.

car model	fast talk	night light	swing low
board bill	step high	down beat	baby buggy

Experience 4

Teacher's Purpose.   To discover that meaning is controlled by the order in which a series of modifiers are placed before the noun.

Directions

What is considered handsome in the sentence phrase, *A man's handsome shirt*?

What is considered handsome in the sentence phrase, *A handsome man's shirt*?

Would you say that the meaning changed in the two examples? Explain. What exactly was done to cause this change in meaning? (See purpose) To reinforce this concept, continue working with the following phrases.

beautiful girl's picture   teacher's first name   pretty chilly girl

Experience 5

Teacher's Purpose.   To discover that the adjectives in a series placed before the noun take the order of number, size and then color.

Directions

Add a word to the word *books* that will tell how many books.

Six books   Several books   Many books   Few books

Now add a word to the phrase that would tell the color. (*Six red*) Now add a word that would give the size of the books? (*Six big red books*) . . . Was there any other order that you would want to arrange these adjectives? (No) Why? Did you say "it wouldn't sound right"? The order in which you placed the adjectives sounds right because it is the way this sequence is used in the English-speaking community; therefore, learning a rule is not necessary for the native speaker. The rule would have to be known, however, in order to help someone learn English.

Variation

Make a list of words under the classification of number, color, and size. Use one of each with a noun of your choice. Test these phrases that were constructed intuitively against the principle of adjective word order being studied. This is the way that linguists work in studying language. Write a principle of word order that would help a friend from another country learn English.

Variation

On the basis of the rule you discovered above, how would you explain what was wrong in the following examples?

Three gray big elephants
Many pink huge balloons
Small several clowns

Experience 6

Directions

Put your knowledge of word order to work in the following sentences. Can you change the meaning?

I'd rather fight than switch.
I'd rather diet than get fat.
It's better to be wise than stupid.
It's better to be safe than sorry.

How many possibilities can you get out of the following sentence?

The tired teachers called over the tall boys.

The overtired teachers called the tall boys.
The tall teachers called the tired boys over.
The tall boys called over the tired teachers.

There are many more. Keep going until you get overtired or over!

UNIT 3.
USING WORD FORM

Previous units pointed out that meaning was controlled by the words and the order in which words were put in a sentence. This unit will demonstrate that the form of the word is also a factor in meaning.

Experience 1

Teacher's Purpose.   To discover that inflectional endings on nouns and verbs can add facts to a sentence just as words do.

Directions

Read the following sentence. How many facts do you find?

The boys are playing.

The obvious facts are: Who is playing? (The boy) What is the boy doing? (Playing) There are two other facts, however, that are signalled by structural endings rather than by the words in the sentence. They can be revealed by asking the questions: How many boys? (More than one) When did he play? (Now) What signals give you this information? (Plural form *s* and present form of verb) You have four facts now instead of two. For example, if each fact in the sentence under study were written separately, you would have:

Who and what?   (The *boys play*)
How many boys?   (More than one boy)
When?   (The boys *are playing now*).

The syntactical signals but not the words were changed in the following sentence:

The boy played.

What facts were changed? (One boy, past tense) What could you say about the use of *word form* as a controller of meaning? (See purpose.)

Variation

Rewrite the following sets of facts, changing the word form only. Do not make any changes in words or word order.
1. The boy talk.
   There more than one boy. The boy not talking now but yesterday.
   (The boys talked.)
2. The dog bark.
   There just one dog. He not barking today but tomorrow.
   (The dog will bark.)
   Which way would you prefer to write your sentences? Do you agree that inflectional endings are efficient items to have?

Experience 2

Teacher's Purpose.   To discover that the possessive form (*'s*) adds a complete fact to the sentence.

Directions

Read the sentences below. Rewrite by combining the facts of the two sentences into one.

The shaggy dog came to school.
The dog belong to boy.

You had no difficulty in producing *The boy's shaggy dog came to school*. Again, you used a special ending called the possessive to do this. The (*'s*), then, is not just a symbol that represents a sound; but it has a meaning that is equivalent to many words.

Variation

Build sentences with the following sets of facts by using your knowledge of noun, verb and possessive forms.
1. The cat is here.
   There is more than one cat. (The cats are here.)
   The cat belongs to Mary. (Mary's cats are here.)
2. The girl walks to the store.
   The girl does not walk today but in the past. (The girl walked to the store.)
   The store belongs to Mr. Smith. (The girl walked to Mr. Smith's store.)
   There is more than one girl. (The girl's walked to Mr. Smith's store.)
How did you express the idea of time, number and possession? Did you need extra sentences? What did you need? (See purpose.)

Experience 3

Teacher's Purpose.   To discover that facts can be added to sentences by using different endings on adjectives.

Directions

Read the set of sentences below. Combine the facts of both sentences into one by using the principle of adjective word form.
1. Fred wore his bright tie.
   No tie in his wardrobe was brighter. (*Fred wore his brightest tie.*)
2. This book is heavy.
   The other book is not as heavy. (*This book is heavier than the other book.*)

Experience 4

Teacher's Purpose.   To discover that inflectional endings standing alone in a sentence string can communicate specific facts.

Directions

Remembering that word endings supply facts (or substitute for whole sentences), what facts do you read in the following sentence strings that are written with inflectional signals only?

1. The ___(1)___ s(2)   ___(3)___ ed(4).

The someone or something (1) of which there is more than one (2) did something (3) that was performed in the past (4).

2. ___ 's(3)   ___(1)(2)___   will(5)   ___(4)___   est(8)   ___(6)___ s(7).

Someone or something (1) in the singular (2) that belongs to someone (3) will do something (4) in the future (5) to something (6) in the plural (7) that can be described to the highest degree (8).

(Note: The reason for using (2) where there is no inflectional ending in Sentence 2 above could be questioned. The absence of an ending signals singular form. This is similar to the zero concept in math.)

Variation

Write your own signal sentences as described above. Share with classmates and read aloud.

Experience 5

Teacher's Purpose.   To develop the ability to analyze the many structural elements that work together to signal the meaning of a sentence.

Directions

Dig into the comprehension of the following sentence by answering the questions that follow. After you do this, determine what syntactical element was used to structure the facts in one sentence.

The most incorrigible boy slid down the elephant's trunk.

What part of the sentence tells

1. Who slid down? (Word order; first slot in sentence.)
2. What the boy did? (Word order; follows subject noun.)
3. How the boy was described? (Word order; placed before noun.)
4. How the elephant was described? (Same as (3))
5. How many boys there were? (Word form; singular.)
6. When the boy slid down? (Word form; past tense ending.)
7. To whom the trunk belonged? (Word form; possessive.)
8. To what degree the boy was incorrigible? (Word form; superlative.)

Variation

Write expanded sentences based on any of the basic patterns and analyze them in the same way as you did the sentence in Experience 5 above.

Variation

Express all the facts in the following sentence as though the English language did not have inflectional endings.

Mary borrowed the teacher's books.

(Mary borrow the book.)
(Borrow not now but before *or* Borrow yesterday.)
(There more than one book.)
(Book belong to teacher.)
Write your own sentences and analyze them in the same way.

Variation

Express all the facts in the following sentence as though the English language did not have the system of word order. To do this, use the symbol # to signal objective case and the symbol * to signal nominative. The modifying adjective would then carry the symbol of the word it modifies.

The upper grade students saw the science projects.

A possibility would be: The students* project# saw the science# upper grade*. Continue this by writing your own sentences and then rewriting with symbols instead of word order.

Variation

Rewrite the following sentences using the English word order.
    The cat* canary# swallowed a.
    Makes haste* waste#.
    The policeman* drivers# speeding# young* caught many#.

Variation

Shift the symbols in the above sentences. What does this do to the meaning?

Examples of Children's Work with Syntactical Signals

The following example was intended to show a world without grammatical signals. Hopefully, as a result of the viewing, the audience will look upon the knowledge of these signals as a privilege rather than as a bore.

Place:	Somewhere; a school.
Characters:	The teacher, students and Signa Grammatica, a newcomer.
Teacher	Where is the book? The book is red. The book belong to Cyrus.
Student	I have the book. The book is red. The book belong to Cyrus. (Enter Signa Grammatica. What kind of person is he(she)? That is up to you to determine.)
Teacher	(frightened) Oh dear! Who you?
Student	You a student? The student new?
Signa	No, I come help you.
Student	You come? You come now, not before? You help? You help now?
Signa	Yes, you take too long to say the simplest thing. I will give you some remarkable shortcuts.
Student	You give shortcut? The shortcut remarkable? You give _____.
Signa	(interrupting) Yes, you have the idea. Let's get started before I waste a full century listening to you. (He takes out a sign on which is printed an *S*.) Here's a sign. That's my first name, you know. *Signa* is Latin for *sign*. When you want to express the idea that there is more than one of anything, just attach this [s] to the word and it will say all that for you.
Teacher	Let me try. The rule. There more than one rule.
Signa	Wait!
Teacher	Oh, I forgot to use the signal. I try again. The rule*S*. (Turns to student.) You know that mean more than one rule.
Student	This sound great. I like shortcut. I mean shortcut*S*. It save so much writing. Do you have more shortcuts?
Signa	Of course. Now here's an *ED*. (Holds up sign and gives to teacher.) This signal expresses the idea that something happened in the past.
Student	Something happen. Not now but before.
Teacher	Say, "Something happen*ED*." Here, use this signal.
Student	It happen*ED*. I walk I walk*ED*. I talk I talk*ED*. I climb I climb*ED*.
Teacher	Enough. Enough.
Student	I want signal. I want more than one.
Teacher	Say it properly. I want signal*S*. The *S* means more than one.
Student	I want signal*S*. I want*ED* signals.

Signa	I have many more signals which I will share with you. Just take care of them and use them well.
Student	I thanked you.
Teacher	You mean, I thank you.
Student	I thank you. I thanked you. Signals fun to use.
Signa	Remember this. People invent things every day. Now we have a new language invention. (Signa exits)
Student	(to teacher) We call this new invention after Grammaticus?
Teacher	Yes, all studentS in the future know it as grammar.

UNIT 4.
EXPANDING SIMPLE SENTENCES

Teacher's Purpose. To discover that new facts can be added to a sentence by using words or groups of words that identify or qualify the naming word in the sentence. Grammatical terminology can be avoided when working with children by using the word itself rather than the generic term for the word. See the example below.

Directions

Read the following sentence and answer the questions.

The boy threw the ball.

What kind of boy do you see? (It doesn't tell.) Could you add words or groups of words that would help to see a particular boy? (big, fat, eight-year-old, teenage, etc.) These words helped you see a particular boy. Now add words or groups of words that could help you see a particular ball. (beach, red, big.) Choose one of your suggested words for each naming word and compose a new sentence.

The teen-age boy threw the big ball. The eight-year-old boy
threw the beach ball.

Did you change the kind of boy or the kind of ball by changing these words? (Yes) Did you change the basic sentence in any way? (No) What exactly did you do? (Check with purpose.) Write your basic sentence again but this time write each fact that you added as a separate sentence and not as an expansion of the same sentence.

The boy threw the ball. The boy was eight years old.
The ball was a beach ball.

Which way would you prefer to write the sentence? (The first way. It doesn't take as long. It sounds better.)

Competency in composing is achieved by producing many original sentences in the various patterns. To do this, make substitutions for the nouns and verbs (naming and doing words) in the models below and then make expansions. (When presenting this to young children, ask them to substitute for underlined words of your presented model.)

The children play.

The teacher met her class.

Our president was George Washington.

The animals are ferocious.

Variation

Blanks are provided for modifying words in the story below. Supply words that will help make the underlined words more precise. When you finish, illustrate your story. Remember that the illustration must agree in every way with the words that were supplied. If the illustration and the words do not agree, then either the word or the drawn detail must be changed until the agreement is perfect.

The _____ Pet

Once upon a time, a dog was very _____. He belonged to a(an) _____ boy who lived in a(an) _____ house on the edge of a(an) _____ town. The _____ boy loved his _____ dog very much and fed him _____ food very faithfully.

One _____ day the _____ dog disappeared. The _____ boy whistled and called desperately. His _____ friends hunted constantly. The _____ boy put a(an) _____ ad in the _____ paper which read as follows: A(An) _____ puppy with _____ hair is lost. His ears are _____ and _____ but his tail is _____. He has a(an) _____ spot on his _____ face. His disposition is _____ and he eats _____ food.

The _____ boy waited a(an) _____ week but not one answer did he get. You see, in that _____ town dogs couldn't read.

What can you say about the effect that your added words had on the story? (They make the story more interesting.) In what way? (More exact picture.)

When doing this with children, display their illustrations and discuss the differences caused by using different modifying words. Make a list of these words for study. Some words that resulted from this assignment when tried in a fifth grade classroom were: frisky, mischievous, floppy, shaggy, gloomy, polkadotted, impulsive, gruesome, etc. Obviously, some of these words are to be preferred over others, but the experienced teacher knows that children have a natural inclination to use what the adult might consider silly words. This tendency wears off, however, when the novelty of the experience diminishes.

Experience 2

Teacher's Purpose.   To discover that new facts can be added to a sentence by using words or groups of words that tell where or when an action takes place.

Directions

Read the following sentence and answer the questions.

John pitched the ball.

1. Add a word or group of words that tell where John pitched the ball. (over the fence, in the park, here, etc.)
2. Add a word or group of words that tell when he pitched the ball. (yesterday, before the game, this morning, etc.)
3. Write your basic sentence again and then write each fact as a separate sentence. (John pitched the ball. It was pitched over the fence. It was pitched yesterday.)
4. Write it as an expanded sentence. (John pitched the ball over the fence yesterday.) Is the basic pattern changed? (No) What did you do? (See purpose.)

Experience 3

Teacher's Purpose.   To discover that facts can be added to a sentence by using words or groups of words that tell how an action took place. This does not change the basic pattern.

Directions

Read the following sentence and follow the directions.

The pony ran.

1. Add a word or group of words that tell how the pony ran. (fast, with ease.)

2. Write your expanded sentence and underline the basic pattern. (*The pony ran* with ease.)
3. Is the basic pattern changed? (No)
4. How were facts added? (See purpose.)

Experience 4

Teacher's Purpose.   To discover that units of information that function in various ways can be added to the same sentence without changing the basic sentence pattern.

Directions

Read the sentence below and follow the directions given.

The boys pitched the tent.

1. Add words that will help you see a particular tent. (*Scout* tent)
2. Add words that will help you see a particular group of boys. (*happy*)
3. Add words that will tell you when they pitched it. (*at daybreak*)
4. Add words that will tell you how they pitched it. (*quickly*)
5. Add words that will tell you where they pitched it. (*by the campfire*)
6. Write the basic sentence with the facts added as expansions. Underline the basic pattern. (At daybreak, the happy boys quickly pitched the Scout tent by the campfire.)

Variation

Reverse what you did in expanding the sentence above by crossing out the word or groups of words that perform the following functions.
1. Makes the noun more specific (or describes). (At daybreak the boys quickly pitched the tent, etc.)
2. Tells when the tent was pitched. (The boys quickly pitched the tent, etc.)
3. Tells how the tent was pitched. (The boys pitched the tent, etc.)
4. To tell where the tent was pitched. (The boys pitched the tent.)
Do you have the basic pattern? *No matter how complex a sentence becomes it can always be reduced in this way to the basic pattern.*

In working with children present this cumulative exercise in various sentence patterns. Some models are presented below. Encourage the writing of original sentences, however, by substituting for the words you wish to underline in the models. Working in this way, children gain a feeling for the qualities of *noun-ness* and *verb-ness,* paving the way for the definition. Remember that at all times the discussion of what was done should be as important as the doing. Fill the chalkboards and use colored chalk extravagantly.

Models to begin with:

Several *crayons* were on the floor.

The *monkeys* ate bananas.

Vacations are wonderful.

Hawaii is a *state*.

Examples of Children's Work Using Sentence Expansion

The experiences described here can be called *Spinning Sentences* with younger students, or *Generating Sentences* with the older ones. These examples should make clear why grade level labels can't be attached to these materials. You will note that the same principle, that of expansion, was developed with both age groups but the content of the sentences and the vocabulary used by the teacher in giving directions was adapted to the maturity and experiences of the students.

Spinning a Sentence (First grade)

The turkey ran.

Let me see the turkey. (*The fat turkey ran.*) Tell me where he ran. (*The fat turkey ran into the woods.*) Tell me when. (*The fat turkey ran into the woods yesterday.*) Tell me how. (*Yesterday the fat turkey ran into the woods very fast.*)

The same questions used in first grade in *Spinning Sentences* were asked in seventh grade with the sentence *The students ate lunch.* The results are listed:

1. During the storm *the* excited *students ate* a tasteless *lunch* quickly in the cafeteria.
2. In the cafeteria during the storm, *the* excited and hungry *students* quickly *ate* a delicious *lunch.*
3. *The* excited and hungry *students ate* a tasteless *lunch* in the cafeteria during the storm.
4. *The* teenage *students ate* a hot *lunch* during the storm in the cafeteria.
5. Yesterday, during the storm, *the* excited and hungry teenage *students ate* a typically tasteless hot *lunch* quickly and impolitely here in the cafeteria.

The discussion that followed was lively and centered around the following:

1. The words for expansion could be inserted in various places in the sentence. While there were several possibilities, there were also limitations, as in Sentence 4 (during the storm in the cafeteria).
2. Sentence 5 was enjoyed by the students and analyzed as:
    a. "More than one adjective was used." "Sometimes there were three."
    b. "More than one answer was given to each question." (Yesterday, during the storm).

Examples of Teacher's Work Using Concept of Sentence Expansion in Theme Correction

If this knowledge of expansion is to be transferred to theme writing, the teacher must recognize the skill as she marks papers for revision. A few examples from such teachers will illustrate the good practices that achieve this. The original compositions that appear below are presented with the teacher's remarks in parentheses.

A. Second grade.
My daddy took me to the circus. (Tell me when.) I saw a funny lady. (Why was she funny? Tell me in another sentence.)
Revision: My daddy took me to the circus *on our vacation*. I saw a *funny lady. She had a bumpy nose and her dress shook.*

B. Third grade.
We took a trip from Asbury Park to Bay Head. We saw many things on our ride. (What kind of things? Name some in another sentence.) We saw many boats on the water. (What kind of boats? Let me see them.)
Revision: We took a trip from Asbury Park to Bay Head. We saw many *interesting* things on our ride. *We saw the Coca Cola factory and the place where men catch big fish.* We saw many *beautiful sail* boats and *busy fishing* boats on the water.

C. Fifth grade.
Our class went to the museum. (When? A particular museum?) When we arrived we stopped for lunch. (What kind?) The guide took us through the halls on the first floor and we saw a movie. (What kind of movie? Could you add a word to describe the guide?) Then we went to different areas. (Name some). My favorite sight was the Egyptian mummy. (because)
Revision: Our class went to the *Metropolitan* museum *last Thursday*. When we arrived we stopped for a *quick* lunch. The *pleasant* guide took us through the halls on the first floor and we saw an *educational* movie

that helped us understand our tour. Then we went to different areas *such as the Greek Sculpture, The Armor Room and the Egyptian Wing.* My favorite sight was the Egyptian Mummy *because it was scary but fascinating. It was educational too.*

D. Kindergarten. An experience chart.
We took a walk. (Tell me when). We saw a house (What kind? Where?) The carpenter showed us his tools. (What kind of tools? How did he show them?) We thanked him and came back. (How did we thank him?) Revision: We took a walk *this morning.* We saw the *nice new* house *on the corner.* The *busy* carpenter showed us his *important* tools *very proudly.* We thanked him *politely* and came back.

The theme revision as described above
1. Requires no technical terms but depends on the teacher's ability to ask questions that will evoke expansions that the child already has on the intuitive level. The teacher, however, must be well informed on the technical level in order to recognize the structures and the stages of development.
2. Puts the responsibility for making expansion on the child. The result will be his idea in which he can take some pride. This pride of creation is somehow absent in revisions that require only well punctuated, properly spelled, and neatly written but uninteresting and monotonous sentence patterns.
3. Does not end with the product under study. The idea spirals on to the next theme and to the next child who participates in the discussions.
  Teachers ask, Does this take time? Yes, but how well spent when one considers all the advantages. From a practical standpoint, however, it should be explained that the examples were developed in detail for purposes of illustration. Teachers need not do *every* sentence in *every* theme. Spot sentences could be taken from certain themes and discussed with the class. This is followed by teams or small groups working together for the purpose of finding how they could improve each other's themes by asking questions like the teacher's. In Experience 3, a child said, "We could ask what kind of tricks the horse was doing". Another child said, "We could spin the sentence in this place." Attention, then, was centered on the job of constructing meaning rather than on the subskills of spelling and punctuation.
  This unit on expanding the sentence was designed to explain the native speaker's intuition about grammar in such a way that technical terminology could be avoided. This was done by referring to each unit in an expanded structure in terms of its intended function rather than by its technical label. That is, an expansion like *yesterday* was referred to as a unit that told when an action took place, but not as an adverb.

It is the function of the unit that reveals the meaning and is therefore a more usable fact in developing comprehension skills than the ability to classify the parts of speech. This analysis and ability to explain what one has constructed or wants to construct is the important beginning step in language production. The next goal is to manipulate sentences in a wide variety of ways and to be able to make appropriate choices. This requires a more detailed description of what one does when he composes. This will be done in Unit 5.

UNIT 5.
EXPANDING AND MANIPULATING COMPLEX
AND COMPOUND STRUCTURES

Units 1–4 expanded sentences in a general way in that the learner supplied expansion units intuitively by answering questions that answered *where, when, how.* Unit 5 will continue the concept of expansion but will analyze more specifically each expansion structure. Again, note that in working with less mature students simply refer to the function intended and not to the terms given the function. For example, in discussing the phrase, *the ugly screaming witches,* refer to *ugly* as *the word that describes the witch* and not as an *adjective.*

The expansion of a sentence element is called clustering in that all the modifying elements cluster around or modify the headword being modified. The ultimate goals for these exercises are to enable the student to:

1. Recognize that the basic sentence patterns form the framework from which all complex structures are developed.
2. Understand how units of meaning are arranged to make a sentence.
3. Construct a variety of clustering structures.
4. Recognize the many choices a writer has when he creates.

Expanding the Sentence by Clustering the
Noun and Verb Headwords*

Experience 1

Teacher's Purpose.   To discover that the noun headword can be modified by units placed before the noun headword. These units modify the

---

* Refer to Section Three of this handbook for a full description of structures which appear before and after noun and verb headwords.

noun in various ways, depending on the intent or function of each. (See Section Three for full description of these clusters.)

Directions

Construct a cluster before the italicized word in the following sentence by adding the facts requested.

The bride wore a gown.

Add these facts: *The gown is long. The gown is trailing. It is made of satin.* By adding the three sentences to the first, did you get *The bride wore a long trailing satin gown?*

Note that each fact that was added to the clustering structure modified the headword in very different ways. For example, in the first sentence,

1. The word *long* functioned as an adjective in that it expressed a quality.
2. The word *trailing* functioned as a verb in that it expressed what the gown was doing. (Note that word order prevents its being the main verb.)
3. The word satin is a noun because it is the material from which the gown is made. (*The gown is made of satin,* not *The gown is satiny.*)

Traditional grammar would describe all these units as adjectives which by definition describe or point out. The relationship between the modifier and the headword is not merely showing quality or pointing out. Knowing what a sentence means depends on determining whether the modifying units function as noun, verb, adjective, or adverb. For example, the sequence *the fair price* could mean the price for the fair, in which case *fair* functions as a noun. It could also mean that the price is moderate or acceptable, in which case *fair* functions as an adjective. In another example, *Our class saw a moving picture,* the word *moving* would function as a verb if the picture were a moving one and not a still. It would function as an adjective if the picture evoked emotion.

Try the same exercise with this sentence and the questions that follow.

The men saved the house.

1. Of what materials is the house made? (stucco, brick etc.)
2. What quality does the house possess? (new, big, old etc.)
3. What is the house doing? (burning, crumbling etc.)

Discuss in terms of purpose. In clarifying the discussion, note that the intent is made clear when each fact is put in a separate sentence as: *The house was made of brick. The house was burning. The house was old.*

Variation

Combine the sentences in each set of sentences below by clustering the italicized headword. When you finish, discuss the function or intent of each word in the cluster.

1. The *test* was difficult. It was for Math. It had been postponed. (The postponed Math test was difficult.)
2. The carpenter built a *room*. It was large. It was for sewing. (Think carefully about this one. Is it a room that sews or a room for sewing?)
3. She has a *coat*. It is mink. It is sheared. It is new.
4. Carol bought a *lamp*. The lamp was for a table. The lamp was antiqued. (Note that the lamp is not an antique but is antiqued. Big price difference!)
5. The *wind* blew the branches. The wind was howling. It was strong.
6. *Children* are playing. Not these children but those. They are happy.

Variation

Test the relationship or intent of meaning of each modifying word in the clusters above by putting them in a *who* or *which* frame as described below.

noun cluster	*clause test*	*functions as*
interesting lesson	which was interesting (Don't let the *ing* ending fool you into calling it a verb)	adjective
complete reducing plan	which is for reducing (*not* which is reducing)	noun
	which is complete	adjective
small dining room	which is small	adjective
	which is for dining	noun
	(which is dining?)	*ing* verb?

Variation

Read the expanded sentences. Write each fact supplied by the noun cluster as a separate sentence. Discuss the intent of each sentence.

1. The witches served the *bubbling, poisoned, magic brew*.
2. Ken has a *red, itching, contagious* rash.
3. The man hired the *large, new moving van*. (Watch this. Was the van moving?)

Modification after the noun is found in more mature writing; and according to studies, the structure presents a formidable comprehension block to reading. This could be because the unit interrupts the main idea by separating the noun from the main verb. In addition, it may be because the reader confuses the verb of the clause with the main verb. Whatever the explanation, it seems reasonable that a simplified explanation of how the structure and its variations work might not only extend its use to a wider group of students but also make it possible to place it earlier in the curriculum. Traditional grammar treats the variations as appositives, adverbials, participials, relative clauses. Instead, the structure can simply be perceived as merging two sentences into one in patterned ways. (See description of structure after the noun headword in Section Three.)

Experience 2

Teacher's Purpose. To discover that a noun headword can be modified by the use of the *who clause* (relative clause.) which follows the noun headword.

Directions

Rewrite the following clusters so that the modifying words that appear before the noun headword appear in the relative clause pattern.
1. The shouting and tumbling cheerleaders _____ (who were _____ and _____).
2. The funny and colorful clowns _____ (who were _____ and _____).
3. The overboiled and tasteless coffee _____ (which was _____ and _____).
4. The cranky, scolding teacher _____ (who was _____ and _____).

Discuss according to purpose.

Experience 3

Teacher's Purpose. To discover that the relative clause can be shortened by inserting the comma and dropping the *who* (which, etc.) *were* (was) part of the clause.

In the revised sentences written above, strike out the clause signal (who, which, etc.) and the verb. The products should resemble this:

The cheerleaders, who were shouting and tumbling.

Read aloud. Read both versions. Note the distinct pause that seems to take the place of the eliminated words. Continue this with all the sentences until you get a feel of the intonation pattern. Since these are just sentence clusters, they need material to complete the sentence.

Write a complete sentence using the cluster in the subject.

Write a complete sentence using each cluster in the predicate. Example:

The coffee, overboiled and tasteless, was thrown out.
The coffee, which was overboiled and tasteless, was thrown out.
The customers bought the coffee which was overboiled and tasteless.

Experience 4

Teacher's Purpose.   To discover that a noun headword can be modified by the use of a prepositional phrase (a group of words starting with *like, in, of, to*) placed after the headword.

Directions

Complete the relative clauses in the following clusters, by supplying the information requested.

1. The astronauts who were *in* _____. (Where were they?)
2. The ball which was *over* _____. (Where?)
3. The drive which was *for* _____. (What?)
4. The information which is *in* _____. (Where?)

When you complete this, strike out the clause signal (who, which, etc.). Read aloud. Read both versions. Were your sentences like this example?

The astronauts who were in the spaceship _____.
The astronauts, ~~who were~~ in the spaceship _____.

Complete the sentence. Example: The astronauts, in the spaceship, checked the signals.

Variation

Check the relationship of the above modifying structure to the headword by writing the same information *before* the headword. Some of the results may sound awkward but the intent of meaning will be clear. Examples are: *The in the spaceship astronauts . . . The for Cancer drive . . .*

Experience 5

Teacher's Purpose. To discover that a noun headword can be modified by the use of the adverb denoting place inserted after the headword.

Directions

Read the following noun headword followed by a relative clause.

The students who are here _____.

Strike out the clause signal, *who are.* Finish the sentence. Do you have: *The students /here/ will eat lunch?*

Discuss in terms of purpose. Does *here* mean that they will *eat here* or that the *students are here?* This distinction is important.

Continue the above exercise with these clusters. Complete the sentences.

1. The newspapers which are inside _____.
2. The decks which are below _____.
3. The classes which are upstairs _____.
4. The campsite which is there _____.

Experience 6

Teacher's Purpose. To discover that a change in structure creates a change in intonation. This intonation influences the mood or style and gives different emphasis to the communication.

Directions

Read these versions of a sentence aloud and listen to the pauses and pitch levels of each sentence. Ask yourself if you feel a difference in the tone of each sentence. Which do you prefer? Why?

The sad, miserable, marching children stopped for lunch.

The marching children, who were sad and miserable, stopped for lunch.

The marching children, sad and miserable, stopped for lunch.

What if you changed your basic sentence pattern to:

The marching *children* who stopped for lunch
were sad and miserable.

Discuss: Did you have the same information? Did the rearrangements give more emphasis to one part than given to another? Explain. Elicit the idea that facts in the main part of the sentence gain more importance than those in modifying structures.

Variation

Choose any expanded sentence pattern and change the modification clusters as described. Work in teams and listen to each other. Can you describe the differences?

In working with sentences in this way, some children confuse the elements of the cluster with the basic sentence as in:

1. *The* baby *skunk* which smelled *was at the school fair.* (original)
2. *The* smelly baby *skunk was at the school fair.* (acceptable alternate)
3. *The* smelly *skunk* which was a baby *was at the school fair.* (acceptable alternate)
4. *The* smelly *skunk* which was at the school fair *is a baby.* (not acceptable. Note change in basic pattern.)

Sentence 4 is acceptable as a sentence but it should not be confused with the noun cluster which is part of the total pattern. If the student confuses these principles then modification structures are not clear to him, and he is apt to suffer with writing sentence fragments.

Experience 7

Teacher's Purpose.   To discover that sets of information can be clustered in various ways on both sides of the headword.

Directions

By using the structures which have been described, combine in various ways the sets of information given below. Underline the basic sentence pattern of each sentence.

1. The girls will sing.
   They belong to the glee club.
   The girls are talented.
   The girls are in the room.

   Watch out for sequences like:
   The talented girls who will sing in that room are in the glee club.
   Ask: What was the intent of the phrase *in the room?*

2. All the lions were hungry.
   The lions were in the parade.
   They were roaring.

   Watch out for sequences like:
   who were roaring in the parade!

3. The boys played baseball.
   They were on the school team.
   They were in Jr. High School.

Variation

After writing the sentences in the above exercise, strike out structures in answer to questions based on the intent of each. For example, in Sentence 1 strike out the part that tells where the girls are (in the room etc.). When all the modification units have been removed in this way, only the basic pattern should remain.

Experience 8

Teacher's Purpose. To discover that the verb headword can be modified but units that supply the information telling how, when or where something is done. While there is some flexibility in the placement of these modifying units there are conditions under which certain word order is mandatory. (See Section Three for a full description of clustering structures.

Directions

Cluster the verb in the following sentence by answering the questions that follow.

The team won.

1. How did they win? (easily, with ease, etc.)
2. When did they win? (yesterday, this morning, in the morning, etc.)
3. Where did they win? (here, in the park, etc.)

Write several sentences on the chalkboard and compare the structures presented by each. Note that some expressed the answer in one word, e.g., *easily,* while others used more than one word, e.g., *with ease.* Also note that answers were placed in various positions in the sentence.

Variation

Write the elements of the basic sentence used in Experience 8 on two sheets of paper. (The team   won.) Choose a set of the clustering units presented by the class in the same experience and write on separate sheets of paper. For example, use *yesterday* or *in the park.* Distribute these to members of the class. Direct those holding the parts of the basic pattern to stand in front of the class and display the complete sentence. Call each card holder in terms of a function, e.g., tells when, etc., to join the sentence and to stand in whatever position in the sentence he prefers. The completed sentence might be

The team (easily) won (in the park) (yesterday).

Many students will readily see that there are several choices for the position of the clusters. Continue to manipulate in this way but be alert to the tendency to compose, *Yesterday the team in the park won easily.* In this arrangement, *in the park* modifies *team* and not the verb.

Continue the exercise described in Experience 8 using these sentences.

> The cat swallowed the canary.
> The white mice escaped.

Experience 9

Teacher's Purpose.   To discover that the position of the modifying structure can change the meaning of the sentence.

Directions

Consider the intent of the underlined words in the following sets of sentences. Is it the same in each? Discuss in terms of the purpose.

1. Mary, who is now my best friend, will get the prize.
   Mary, who is my best friend, will get the prize now.
2. The books in the library will be checked out today.
   The books will be checked out in the library today.

Variation

Test the placement of verb clusters by writing original sentences and testing them as you did above.

Variation

Test the intent of each unit in your clusters by listing the units under the headword that they modify. Note that while this method may at first seem like traditional diagramming, it differs basically because it is the complete unit and its intent that is being identified, and not the classification of each word in the unit. Reading and writing require this act of thinking in thought units, not in individual words.

The children, in the kindergarten, sang songs in assembly yesterday.

Children	*sang*
in the kindergarten	in the assembly
	yesterday.

Variation

Test the intent of each unit in your clusters by color coding the units. Work at the chalkboard with lecturer's chalk.

1. The girls in the room, who are talking and giggling, will report to the principal's office tomorrow.
2. The man on the highest trapeze will perform fantastically in the finale.
3. The reading teachers downstairs complained every day.

Expanding the Sentence by Using Subordination

The ability to write with control of subordinating structures is one of the most advanced skills on the sentence continuum. Because the structure is used in many of the content area textbooks it presents a formidable comprehension block to many readers. It seems advisable, then, for teachers to simplify the description by relating it to intuitive use and to offer many situations in which these structures can be manipulated and discussed. For some children, only the syntactical structure will need to be revealed; for others, the very concept expressed by the subordinators will need to be developed.

Just as several sentences were merged into one by structuring clusters around the headwords, two sentences can be merged by attaching a subordinator. In so doing, a particular relationship of *cause and effect, time, consession, condition,* or *result* is established. This relationship is not present when two sentences stand as separate units. (See Section Three for full description of these structures.)

Experience 1

Teacher's Purpose. To discover that: (1) a particular relationship between sentences is established by the use of subordinating words; (2) this relationship is not present when the sentences stand as independent units.

Directions

Present the sets of sentences that follow. Elicit the idea that each sentence in the set presents a fact but that they are not related. Proceed to link the sentences with various subordinators. As each subordinator is added, encourage students to explain the difference that the subordinator made in the relationship. Encourage the use of their own descriptions rather than the formal labels.

1. Donna finished her homework.
   She ate a Sloppy Joe.

Because Donna finished her homework, she ate a Sloppy Joe. (Cause and effect)

After Donna finishes her homework, she will eat a Sloppy Joe. (Time.)

2. The teacher finished her reports.
   She couldn't leave for her vacation.
   Add: *Although, Before, Until, Unless* (note change in verb forms to do this).
3. Mary's puppy bit the teacher.
   The principal sent it home.
   Add: *After, Because, Since, When.*

Variation

Expand the following sentence by attaching a sentence to the subordinating word which is supplied.

1. Eric wore heavy boots *because*
2. Our teacher will be happy *if*
3. Our experiment failed *when*
4. Roy couldn't find the ball *since*
5. The class must be quiet *before*

After composing the above sentences, change the subordinator and discuss the difference in relationship. For example, sentence 1 could read:

Eric wore heavy boots *until* (*after, when*, etc.).

Variation

Follow the directions in the above exercise but note that in this set the subordinator is placed at the beginning of the first sentence instead of the second.

1. After I did my homework, —————.
2. Because I was lazy, —————.
3. Although I looked through the microscope,—————.
4. If you make a cake, —————.

Variation

Join the following sets of sentences with your choice of a subordinating word. The information in the underlined sentence must be considered the main sentence.

1. The weather was beautiful. John decided to stay indoors.
   (Although the weather was beautiful, John decided to stay indoors.)
2. He enjoyed adventure stories and historical fiction. He enjoyed science fiction most of all.

3. Steve spent the summer in camp. He left immediately for school in the fall.
4. The boys practiced hard. They won the game.

After composing the above sentences, read them aloud. Listen to them structured with the subordinating unit written first and then with the subordinating unit written second. Which version gives more emphasis to the main sentence?

Variation

Substitute for each unit in the following sentences. Do not change the syntax or the subordinating word. Only the content will be changed.

1. Because of the blockade, the farmers in the Mississippi Valley went to see the president.
   (Because of the new rule, the students in our class went to see the principal.)
2. If we had followed the king's orders, we would have had taxation without representation.
   (If Leslie had attended the senior assembly, she would have seen a program without expense.)

Examples of Young Children at Work with Subordinators

Young children can learn to think in these subordinating structures by having guided oral experiences like those described below.

Game: *If*   I will start *If* and you finish.
Examples: If I forget my book _____.
           If school closed _____.
           If I had a wish _____.
           If everyday were a holiday _____.

Variation

Students present the *If* structure and the teacher or other students complete the sentence. For example:
    If it rains today _____.
    If today is Monday _____.
    If I'm good _____.

Variation

Change to a *When* game with such structures as, *When I grow up.*

Variation

Present a page with a subordinating clause dittoed on top. Children finish the sentence orally and then draw a picture of what was said.

Variation

Complex structures can gradually become part of the writing program by structuring frames for the child to complete by substituting. Collate their illustrated sentence frames and put in book form for class reading.

1. A _____ is bigger than I am *but* I am bigger than a _____.
2. A _____ is tall, but a _____ is taller.

Substitute adjectives depending on the concept you wish to develop. It is best to confine choices to regular adjectives for early experiences.

Expanding the Sentence by Compounding and Coordination

The ability to identify the functional units of the sentence, to compound them at will, and to choose from a variety of sentence coordinators is a skill to be valued. Although this skill of multiplying syntactically equivalent elements is familiar to young students, sequential practice in constructing and analyzing these patterns not only reveals awkward structures but also offers options in composing.

Experience 1

Teacher's Purpose. To discover that two sentences with a common predicate can be combined by compounding (joining) the subject nouns of each sentence.

Directions

Read aloud the set of sentences below. How do they sound? (Elicit such observations as *repeats, boring, baby sentences.*)

The trees are sprouting. The bushes are sprouting.

Revise by (1) finding the parts of the sentence that are the same and striking them out; (2) joining the two subject nouns using the word *and*. For example: *The trees are sprouting. The bushes are sprouting.*

The bushes and trees are sprouting.

Work in the same way with these sentences.

1. The teachers are here. The children are here.
2. John saw the astronauts. Russ saw the astronauts.
3. Mrs. Adams is a teacher. Her daughter is a teacher.
4. The superintendent attends the meetings. The parents attend the meetings.

Note: Watch for the change in verb form found necessary in 3 and 4.

Variation

Instead of using the word *and* rewrite the sentences above as well as some original sentences by using *not only/but also* and *both/and*.

Experience 2

Teacher's Purpose. To discover that two adjectives with common head-words can be compounded by joining the adjectives and combining the sentence.

Directions

Combine the sentences in each set by striking out the parts that repeat and joining the adjectives with the word *and*.
1. The apple is sweet. The apple is small. (The apple is small and sweet.)
2. The school is new. The school is popular.
3. The seashore is hot. The seashore is crowded.

Variation

Instead of using the word *and*, use the word *but* in the sentences above. Discuss in terms of the meaning of *and/but*.

(The apple is small but sweet.)

Experience 3

Teacher's Purpose. To discover that two sentences can be combined by joining the complete subjects and attaching the common predicate.

Directions

Proceed as in Experience 1, but now compound the entire subject.
1. The new toys are in the playground.
The special equipment is in the playground.
(The new toys and special equipment are in the playground.)
2. Fresh fruit is healthy.
Green salad is (also) healthy.

Combining subjects in this way can sometimes produce an ambiguous statement. For example, in the combination: *The fifth-grade boys talked. The girls talked.* becomes *The fifth-grade boys and girls talked.* But, did the original statement say that the girls as well as the boys were in the fifth grade? What can be done to make it accurate? (*The girls and the fifth-grade boys talked, or The fifth-grade boys and the girls talked.*)

In classrooms where math is enjoyed, the difference in meaning of the two structures can be compared to the difference in the two formulas: $a(b + c)$ = fifth-grade boys and girls; $ab + c$ = fifth grade boys and the girls.

Variation

Avoiding ambiguity: Combine the following sentence sets into compound structures. Check for ambiguity by referring back to the intent expressed in the original sentences. Explain what you did to avoid unclear compounds.

1. The new cars sped on the turnpike. The motorcycles sped on the turnpike.
2. Pedigreed dogs were in the school fair. Children were in the school fair.
3. The talking parrots were popular. The puppies were popular.
4. The strawberry ice cream melted. The chocolate ice cream (also) melted.

Note: If you compose sentence 4 as *The strawberry and chocolate ice cream melted,* the mathematical formula would be $a + a(b)$ melted. Ask: Am I compounding adjectives or whole subjects in this exercise? How is the meaning of the two structures affected?

Variation

For those who like to make up formulas for structures this can be done by using N = noun; V = verb; a = adjective or modifier; d = determiner; + = compounding structure. (See Section Three for full description.)

Example: d aN + dN   (The crunchy potato chips and the marshmallows.)

d a (N + N)   (The crunchy potato chips and the crunchy marshmallows!)

Variation

Substitute content words for the elements in these formulas. Use the same content words in every formula of the same set. Compare meanings.

1. (d) a(N + N) V   2. (d) aN + aN V
   (d) a N + N V   (d) aaN + N V
   (d) N + aN V   (d) aa(N + N) V
                             (d) N + aaN V

Variation

Substitute the compounding structures

not only/ but also; both/ and; either/or; neither /nor;

for the word *and* in the sentences composed in earlier exercises.

Example: Not only the new cars but also the motorcycles sped on the turnpike.
Both the new cars and etc.
Either the new cars or etc.
Neither the new cars nor etc.

Experience 4

Teacher's Purpose.   To discover that two sentences *with a common subject* can be combined by compounding the predicate verbs of each sentence.

Directions

Follow same procedure as that used for compounding subject nouns.
1. The children played. The children sang. (The children played and sang.)
2. The dog barked. The dog snarled.
3. The clowns jumped. The clowns turned cartwheels.

Variation

Compose compound predicates by following these step-by-step directions. Note that in this method the content of each sentence will be different but the structure remains unchanged.
1. Write a noun phrase. (The team)
2. Add a verb of your choice. (The team lost.)
3. Use the same noun phrase but add another verb. (The team cheered.)
4. Cross out the noun phrase of item 3 and attach the remainder of the sentence to the sentence in item 2. (The team lost and cheered.)

Variation

For those who like to work with formulas, express the compound sentence exercise in formula form. For example:

$$d \; N \; V \text{ and } d \; N \; V$$

combines into

$$d \; N \; V + V$$

Compounding as described here can be used to connect any like constructions in the English sentence. The ability to identify these functional units, to compound them at will and to choose from a variety of conjunctions and coordinators is a skill to be valued. The units in the sentence are listed here as a guide to the teacher who wishes to construct appropriate compounding exercises for his students.

1. Nouns   The parents and teachers
2. Verbs   Ate and left
3. Adjectives   Short and fat
4. Adverbs   Fast and furiously
5. Verb clusters   usually ate early and left for school immediately
6. Prepositional phrases   up the stairs and into the library
7. Sentences   The principal observed the teachers and the teachers observed the children.

Experience 5

When verbs in a string are all alike in form they are called parallel in structure. This pattern is often found in literature or used by expert speakers as it is very expressive and pleasing to the ear. Since it is not a difficult form, young students can develop the art of using it.

Teacher's Purpose.   To discover the parallel structure of verbs.

Directions

Provide frequent oral experiences like this one. Start by saying to the class a sentence like *I am going to swim.* Volunteers from the class must continue with the same verb form but substitute other words, e.g., *I am going to laugh.* After a few sequences have been offered, record them and read aloud in a string, e.g., *I am going to swim, to laugh and to cry.* After the game is understood, any student could start the string with any verb form he prefers. Each time, point out the likeness in the verb forms that follow that of the leader.

Variation

Directed writing of parallel structures: Listen and follow step-by-step directions.

1. Write a noun phrase. (The kindergartners)
2. From the following choose three verbs *written in the same form*: *jumped, hopped, skipped, were jumping, were skipping, were hopping, did skip, did hop, did jump.*
3. Add your verb string to the noun phrase you chose above. (The kindergartners jumped, laughed and hopped.) Read aloud. Listen to those read by volunteers from the class.
4. Use the same three verbs you chose in 2 above. This time mix up the forms and add to your noun phrase. (The kindergartners laughed, were jumping and hopping.)
5. Read this last sentence aloud and compare it to your earlier version. Which version do you prefer? Explain.

Variation

Rewriting for parallelism. The verb strings in the practice sentences below are not parallel. Write each verb in the sentence in columnar form as seen in the example. In the second column, write each verb in parallel form.

Example: They were swiming, dove and did some practicing on the diving board.

Column form	*Parallel forms*
were swimming	were swimming, diving and practicing
dove	swam, dove and practiced
did practicing	did swimming, diving and practicing

1. He liked camping and to fish for trout.
2. His vacation was for reading and to do some fishing.
3. She liked reading and exciting dates.
4. The teacher ranted, roared and was pleading.
5. She wanted to draw, reading, and hiking.

Variation

Construct formulas for these structures using *Ving, Ved, to V* as elements. (N Ved, Ved and Ved) (N Ving, Ving and Ving)

A Reference for Teachers

UNIT 1.
BASIC SENTENCE PATTERNS

While eight sentence patterns are described here, just the first four or five are most generally used in the elementary school. In fact, if the student can apply the concept of substitution and expansion to just a few of these, this ability will automatically transfer to the more complex patterns. The formula that appears with each pattern uses the following symbols:

N	Noun (or pronoun)	V	Verb
Aj.	Adjective	LV	Linking verb
Av.	Adverb	BV	Verb "to be"
d	Determiner	aux	Auxiliary
( )	Symbol enclosed not essential to pattern		

The exponents are used to clearly point out the syntactical relationships between words in the pattern. Teachers of advanced students may wish to use these symbols in constructing sentences. See below.*

Pattern I   (d) N¹V.
Dogs bark (barked, will bark, are barking, etc.).

This is the simplest pattern and demonstrates the subject-predicate relationship. That is, the verb agrees with the subject noun in number

---

* For those that do, the writer suggests that one basic sentence symbol be written in caps and the modifying structures in lower case. This clearly sets the modifying units apart. For example: The formula for *The studious girls passed the exam easily* is (d) a N^1V d N^2 av.

unless the function is assumed by the auxiliary as in *The dog is barking.* This principle is at the very core of sentence comprehension.

Pattern II   (d) N¹ V (d) N².
The PTA purchased the television.

This is the most frequently used pattern and has the advantage of clearly expressing the concept of *performer, the performing,* and the *object.* It can also be transformed to passive voice by the interchange of the subject and object. In so doing, the subject becomes the object of the preposition *by* and the verb changes to the past participle with the auxiliary. The transformed pattern becomes: N¹ aux Ved *by* (d) N. *The television was purchased by the PTA.* The verbs in this pattern are always transitive, demanding an object. (Note the exponent on the predicate noun.) They are very different from the verbs that are to be introduced in Patterns III and IV.

Pattern III   (d) N¹LV (d) N¹.
Miss Marsh is our teacher.

Here, the function of the verb is not to transfer action from the subject noun to the predicate noun, as it did in Pattern II, but to *link* the subject and predicate nouns. This could be referred to as the equation pattern as the nouns could exchange places without disturbing the meaning. *Miss Marsh is our teacher* could also read *Our teacher is Miss Marsh.*

Pattern IV   (d) N¹LV aj.
Her average seems high.   The sundae is rich.

This is similar to Pattern III in that the verb functions in the same way but the predicate complement is an adjective and not a noun. The adjective can be shifted to the subject position and express the same intent as in *The rich sundae is rich.*

Pattern V   (d) N¹ BV Av (of place).
The guests are here.   The child is on the swing.

This construction is confined to the verb *to be.* Notice that the adverbial can either be a phrase or a single word.

Pattern VI N^1 V N^2 N^3.
The teacher gave John a detention.

This pattern is similar to Pattern II but contains two objects, the direct and the indirect. While the children have little difficulty in Pattern II, they seem to confuse the objects when used in this pattern. A way of identifying the indirect object is to test whether it can follow the preposition *to* or *for*. The example above can be tested by restructuring it as *The teacher gave a detention (to John)*. *John*, then, is the indirect object. The test does not reveal *detention* as the indirect object as one could not say *The teacher gave John (to or for detention)*.

Pattern VII N^1 V N^2 N^2.
The teacher appointed Cathy monitor.
They elected Roy president.

Note carefully that while there are again two nouns in the predicate, these nouns have a different relationship from that in Pattern VI. This is shown in the exponents. The predicate nouns refer to each other and not to the subject noun. That is, *monitor* and *Cathy* are the same and *Roy* and *president* are the same.

Pattern VIII N^1 V N^2 Aj.
She called the student bright.

This is similar to Pattern VIII but the object complement is an adjective rather than a noun. The word *bright* describes *student* but is not the same as *student*.

UNIT 2.
WORD CLASSIFICATIONS

About Nouns or Class I

1. They can be pluralized: *-s* (*books*), *-es* (*matches*) and by internal change (*men*).
2. They have certain derivational endings: *-ment, -ness, -tion, -ity, -ence, -ance*.
3. The endings change to link with the main verb: *The boy runs. The boys run.*

4. They can be signalled by a determiner: *an apple, her man, this paper.*
5. They pattern in certain ways like *apple, beauty, desk.* This means that words that would fit in such sentence frames as the following would be nouns.

The _____ is there.

_____ is _____.

The _____ chased the _____.

The _____ on the _____ chased the _____.

About Verbs or Class II

1. They link with the noun as described above. When the auxiliary is used, however, the agreement is in the auxiliary and not in the verb: *The dog is barking. The dogs are barking.*
2. The form changes to express time: *operate/operated/will operate/is operating.*
3. They can accept a form of *be* as an auxiliary.
4. They cannot be signalled by a determiner.
5. They pattern in certain ways. That is, only verbs would fit in the slots in the following sentence frames.

The play _____ interesting.

She _____ the piano.

She _____.

The school _____ on that street.

About Adjectives or Class III

1. They pattern with intensifiers like *very, most, more.*
2. They take the inflectional endings *-ly* (*queenly*), *-ible* (*terrible*), *-ful* (*frightful*), *-able* (*recognizable*), *-al* (*national*), *-ic* (*dramatic*).
3. They can be used with the noun which they usually precede.
4. They can be preceded by a determiner which is signalling the noun to come.
5. They pattern like *happy, beautiful, good.*

The _____ children are in school.

They seem _____.

About Adverbs or Class IV

1. Most, but not all, *-ly* words are adverbs. (See inflectional endings on adjectives above.)

2. They can pattern in many parts of the sentence.
3. They can pattern with intensifiers: *very cheerfully, most kind, so often.*
4. They pattern like *in, beautifully, often.*

In addition to these four classes, there is a set of approximately 300 structure words which do not tend to grow in number. They have no clear lexical meaning as the class words do, but indicate the structural relationship between the class words. These structure words are grouped here according to their functions.

About Structure Words

1. Determiners.   These signal the noun to come and are often referred to as noun markers. The determiner patterns in any slot in which *the* could be used in a sentence frame. For example, in the sentence *The salary is adequate,* the following list of determiners could substitute: *a/an, your, their, his/her, every, one, all, another, each, every, no, that/those,* etc.
2. Auxiliaries.   These signal the verb to come and are often referred to as verb markers. The auxiliary patterns in any slot in which a verb can be used. A representative list would be: *may, might, would, should, shall, will, can, could, might have, has had, can have, should have,* etc.
     Note that the *to be* verb plays a dual role which probably accounts for the difficulties it presents to many students. In this role as an auxiliary it is a time marker with the main verb. In a sentence like *Our company is here,* it carries the content as the main verb. This distinction must be kept clear.
3. Phrase markers.   These words signal nouns or other nominals.   A representative list would be: *of, over, at, after, like, behind, to, across, on, near, among, during, against, since, up.*
4. Clause markers or subordinators.   These words introduce dependent clauses. A representative list would be: *who, whoever, which, whichever, because, if, while, after, that.*
5. Question markers.   These are words used at the beginning of a sentence to signal a question. They are often referred to as interrogators. They are *What, Where, When, Who, Why, How,* etc.
6. Qualifiers or Intensifiers.   These are words used with the adjective and adverb. A representative list would be: *very, rather, too, somewhat, more, less, quite, most, least.*

7. Coordinators.   These are words which join sentences or parts of sentences. A representative list would be: *and, but, or, so, yet, for, neither, nor*, etc.

UNIT 3.
EXPANSION UNITS

1. Expansion. Adding units of meaning to a basic sentence pattern.
2. Headword. The noun or verb around which modifiers are built.
3. Cluster. The group of structures which modify the headword.
4. Clustering patterns.

The noun headword can be modified both by clustering units before the headword and after the headword. Structures which appear *before* the headword are:
1. One or more determiners. (All those papers)
2. One or more adjectives. (Ugly duckling)
3. Another noun. (leather shoe)
4. The *-ing* verb form. (present participle) (The Singing Nun)
5. The *-ed* verb form. (past participle) (The sprained wrist)

Structures which appear *after* the noun headword are:
1. The relative (or who) clauses introduced by *who, which, that*, etc. (The class met the teacher who is new.)
2. The prepositional phrase introduced by such words as *in, to, for, on, by*, etc. (The first day of this month is Tuesday.)
3. Adverbs which denote place, such as *below, inside, here, upstairs*, etc. (The books upstairs were sold.) Note that the word *upstairs* in this sentence does not tell where the books were sold and therefore does not modify the verb.

The verb headword can be clustered with various structures which are:
1. The adverb of time such as *usually, often, never*, etc. (The teacher *usually* gave homework.)
2. The adverb of manner such as *carefully, awkwardly, easily*, etc. (He opened the package *carefully*.)
3. The adverb of place or direction such as *out, upstairs*, etc. (The boys ran *out*.)
4. The noun phrase performing the adverb function such as *that time, this evening*, etc. (The play will be held *this evening*.)
5. The prepositional phrase performing the adverb function, such as *in the playground, by evening, at night*, etc. (The parents come to school *at night*.)

6. The subordinating clause performing the adverb function.

since, as, when, because	cause and effect
though, although	concession
until, after, before, when, while	time
if, unless	condition
so, therefore	result

UNIT 4.
THE STORY OF PUNCTUATION

Philip looked up from his waxed tablet. The task of copying was a laborious one. If he did well today his tutor, Menton, had promised that he could use the papyrus and ink for the final copy. His tutor looked on and, although he seemed severe, he really understood how much Philip preferred the hours in the gymnasium to those spent in the classroom.

"Remember your father's promise to let you travel to Alexandria," he said. "But you cannot go until you are ready to read the manuscripts in the great library."

"Why can't you read them for me?" asked Philip. "You know father said that you were to accompany me."

"When you go, Philip, it will be as an educated man. That is your father's wish."

Philip returned to his copying only to stop abruptly to ask another question. "Why is it," he said, "that in today's lesson there are no dots placed between the words but in yesterday's manuscript a dot separated one word from the other?"

"That is the style of the scribe," said Menton. "They believe that leaving spaces spoil the appearance of the manuscript so the words are placed together. Some of the scribes try to help the reader by placing a dot between the words. Look for the style when you see the inscriptions on the temple walls. Let us go and examine some of them and while we are there listen to Socrates in the market place. His words will be written in the manuscripts that future students will study, but you will have the privilege of hearing him in person."

You would have had great difficulty reading the manuscript that Philip was copying, not only because it was written in another language but, as Philip said, the words were put together without spaces between them. Try reading the following passage and you will have some idea how difficult reading would be, even in our own language, if there were no spaces between words.

ARENTYOUHAVINGADIFFICULTTIMEREADINGTHIS
ISWHATALLYOURREADINGWOULDBELIKEIFSCHOL

ARSHADNTINVENTEDMETHODSOFDIVIDINGANDM
ARKINGTHELANGUAGE

You can see how it became very necessary to find ways of marking and spacing writing, not only for easier reading but for clearer understanding.

An interesting example of how messages without punctuation could be misunderstood can be found in the story told about the young wife of a Greek warrior who wanted to know whether her husband would be successful in battle. Since in those times it was the custom to consult the oracle, she went to Mt. Olympus and asked what the fate of her husband would be. The oracle answered and the woman was very happy. As you read it, make sure that you pause at the commas.

Ibis, redibus, nunquam in bello peribis.

You will go, you will return, never in war will you perish.

She said goodbye to her husband, confident that she would see him again. Time passed and legions returned, but her husband was not among them. Wondering, she went again to the oracle and complained that her husband had not returned. "You failed in your prophesy," she said angrily.

The oracle then corrected her and said, "The prophesy was correct but read improperly. I wrote

Ibis, redibus nunquam, in bello peribus.

You will go, you will return never, in war will you perish."

This time you will notice that the pause was put in another place. Do you agree that there was a big change in the meaning?

In an effort to avoid such mistakes, the scribes introduced marks in the manuscripts that would aid the reader. These differed from the punctuation marks that we know today. Three dots, called *distinctiones*, were placed at different levels to signal different breath lengths. One placed high in the space (•) was similar in meaning to our period and indicated opportunity to recover breath. The dot placed in the middle of the space (•) indicated a short pause, and a dot placed on the line (₌) meant pause very little for not many words remained to be spoken. This system of marking continued for several centuries.

One day in the first century B.C. slaves were gathered outside the museum of Alexandria. They awaited their young masters who gathered to study the great manuscripts with learned scholars.

"What is all the excitement today?" asked one.

"My master's tutor told me that there was to be a great grammar scholar here today."

"Yes", said another, "It is Dionysius of Thrax. My master said he has written the first grammar. His manuscript is as important to grammar as Euclid's manuscript is to the study of geometry."

"It would have to be great indeed," said another.

And it was, for the grammar of Dionysius was the model for language texts for a long time and his ideas in punctuation were followed by many scribes. While Dionysius composed some rules of punctuation, scholars experimented with various kinds of marks. The dots in different positions, the distinctiones, were used by many scribes, but gradually the marks as we use them today developed in interesting ways.

The Period

The period, one of the earliest marks, was originally a circle (o) representing the Greek word *Periodos* (*peri*–all around; *odos*–the way). Freely translated it meant that an idea had been completed or a thought had been gone around. This circle gradually became a dot and has remained so to this very day. While the period was used to separate sentences, the capital letter to start new sentences was not introduced until the Christian era. If you had visited a scriptorium where manuscripts were prepared you would have seen that the regular scribes did not make these capital letters. They referred them to the rubricator who colored these special letters red (rubrus). Because these letters were much taller than the rest they were called uncials, which meant inch high. It is said that St. Jerome gave this exaggerated name to them because they seemed to him to be an inch high.

The Question Mark

In our language we sometimes express questions by changing the order of words; for example, "You will go" to "Will you go?" In Latin, this could not be done. To express a question, the signals *Ne* or *Quaestio* were used to mean, *read this as a question.* If, for example, a Roman boy wanted to trade some marbles, he would say, *"Trade some marbles quaestio."* When you saw the word *quaestio,* you would know that it meant the same as "Will you trade some marbles?" The Roman student soon found some shortcuts for this word; and instead of writing *Quaestio,* he would write just the first and last letters, *Qo.* Gradually the *o* was placed under the *Q.* The *o* finally became a dot and the mark became (⁇). You can see how similar this is to our modern question mark.

The Exclamation Mark

The history of the exclamation mark is very similar to that of the question. The word *Io* was used at the end of a sentence to express a strong feeling. *Io* would be the equivalent to the words *wow!* or *oh!* today. Can't you now see how this became the modern exclamation mark? The *o* shifted back under the *I*. The *o* became a dot (!) and there it was for us to use as "!".

Quotation Marks

The quotation marks that you use are another short cut started by the Romans. At first they used the word *Quotus* which meant *to speak.* A message would be stated like this: *Diana said, Quotus I will meet you at the Forum Quotus.* Then, to save time, instead of writing *quotus* they drew lips to represent the idea of speaking. Now the message would be written like this: Diana said ➤ *I will meet you at the Forum.*◀

You can see how the lips could become the two small hooks that we use today.

The Comma

And the comma? Dionysus of Thrax set up rules about sentences that could be divided into parts. These divisions were shown by a slanted line (/) called a *komma.* This word meant *cut into parts.* The line gradually was shortened into the mark that we call the comma today, and it still divides the sentences into parts.

Although these *marks* were invented, there was no set of rules for their use. Scribes put them in according to personal preference and often with the idea of aiding dramatic reading. More care was taken for end marks than for the comma; and if a mistake were made, a scribe would hesitate to make a correction because the appearance of his manuscript was more important to him than the punctuation.

All this experimenting with punctuation took many, many centuries. During this time comparatively few books were written and these were done by a few people, the scholars and the scribes. Suddenly, something happened that was to make a great change. The printing press was invented. Now punctuation was not the concern of a small group but of an ever-growing number of people. It was the printers who faced the very practical problem that had to be solved quickly. Type was expensive.

They couldn't possibly make the variety of styles that were in use. But in what style should the printers' type be made? Aldus Manutius, the owner of the famous Aldine press in Italy, called the printers together to agree on the design of the marks and the rules for their use. It is their designs and rules with which we are familiar today.

It took years, however, for those rules to be known. Remember that news did not travel fast at that time and a comparatively small number of people attended school. Because the Aldine Press was in Italy, the punctuation practices became more uniform there, but there is evidence that these rules were not widely applied in England even as late as the seventeenth century. Some examples can be seen in quotations from Shakespeare's plays that were first published in 1623.

> Sleeping, and walking, oh defend me still.
> We will unite the White, and the Red

You probably would never use the comma in the same places. Read them again with distinct pauses at each comma. You read slowly, don't you? Don't you feel the dramatic emphasis given to the words as Shakespeare's printers grouped them? Because Shakespeare wrote primarily for actors, it can be understood why different Shakespearean scholars would argue over the way they thought Shakespeare meant a particular passage to be punctuated. Since his plays were not published until several years after his death they could not go to him directly to find out. Some day you may find it very interesting to read the *Variorum Shakespeare*, a text of his plays which shows the different punctuation used in different editions. Read the famous quotation from *Hamlet* that is punctuated four different ways on this page. Can you feel the power of the different styles of acting based on this difference in punctuation?

> To be, or, not to be.   That is the question.
> To be or not to be?   That is the question.
> To be, or not to be.   That is the question?
> To be or not to be.   That is the question!

Which way would you choose to act it out? Why? As you hear the different tone and rhythm do you visualize another kind of man?

As more people went to school and news was carried over the continent more quickly, writers followed more closely the rules set down by Manutius. But it wasn't long before scholars disagreed about these rules. One grammarian would say, "Oh you must absolutely put a comma before the final *and* in a series." Another would say, "This is nonsense. I can prove that this comma isn't necessary." Today scholars are proving that they were both right and both wrong in their arguments.

There are interesting stories in which the comma features. One is about a comma that was left out in a sentence. This is how it happened. An early tariff bill placed a duty on certain fruits that came into the United States. It read as follows:

A duty of _____ shall be placed upon all the following fruits coming into the United States: the orange, pear, pineapple, banana apple,—. What happened? A duty was collected on oranges, pears, pineapples and the banana apple but all the bananas and other kinds of apples came in free. This cost the government $27,000 before they discovered the mistake and put a comma between banana and apple.

This next example has not cost money but it does show a shift in meaning in one of our well known Christmas carols. The phrase, *God Rest Ye, Merry Gentlemen,* said now as though we were addressing *the merry gentlemen,* was originally written *God Rest Ye Merry, Gentlemen.* "God Rest Ye Merry" was an English equivalent to our *goodnight* or *sleep well.*

You might now find it interesting to change the punctuation of a few sentences and discover how these changes affect the meaning.

Shall we eat, father, before you leave?
Shall we eat father before you leave? (Which sentence might give you indigestion?)

"Johnny," said his mother, "is only six years old."
Johnny said his mother is only six years old. (Who was six years old?)

Did you notice that when you read each pair of examples that your voice paused and went up and down at different places?

There is a group of scholars, called linguists, who say that we express meaning not only by the words that we use but by the change of tone of our voice and the accent and pauses that we put in our speech. Punctuation marks, they say, are the written signals for the accents, pauses and change of tone that we use in the spoken language. You might say that they are the marks that show the melody and rhythm of our language as music notes show the melody and rhythm of a song.

Because the punctuation marks are signals that tell us how to read the communication, many writers and student decide on how to punctuate a piece of writing by thinking about what he wants the reader's voice to do. This system helps these writers more than memorizing rules. To practice this idea, read the following sentences, listening carefully to the melody and rhythm of your voice. Especially notice how the punctuation marks guide what you do.

The fat lady thinks that man is the biggest attraction in the circus.
The fat lady, thinks that man, is the biggest attraction at the circus.
(Who is the biggest attraction?)

"Bob," yelled Jim, "stay away from me."
Bob yelled, "Jim, stay away from me." (Who yelled?)

Why is it long?
Why? Is it long?

While the use of punctuation marks has changed through the years, the important idea remains. That is that they are very important in helping us write what we mean. We must use the mark that will help our readers know what we want to say.

You agree that punctuation marks are fun and important? Punctuation marks are fun and important. Punctuation marks are fun and important!

Chapter Four

When English Is a Second Language

English is unquestionably a second language for the non-native speaker who must learn a new language in all its aspects—the vocabulary, the phonology and the syntax. It is also a second language, however, for a large number of our children who use the non-standard dialect of either a regional or minority group. The Pidgin of Hawaii, the Creole of Louisiana, the Mountain Speech of the Appalachians and Ozarks, the farmer of the midwest, the Afro-American and the Spanish centered in our large cities, and the American Indian on the reservations are examples. While these children speak *English*, their phonology, syntax, idiomatic expressions and background experiences differ to such a degree from the standard English of the classroom that their difficulties are comparable to those found in learning a new language. They have an added handicap, however, in that the language problem of the non-native speaker is recognized as an acceptable explanation for his learning block and is treated accordingly, while the divergent speaker, because his language resembles English, has been forced to learn or rather fail to learn in standard English, a language virtually foreign to him. Country-wide surveys give us glaring evidence that these children are the non-achievers who suffer the fate of the academic dropout. They make up a large percentage of the groups labeled as the illiterate, the slow learner, the remedial, the non-promoted, the discipline problems, and the non-employable. No wonder that language divergence, so closely associated with these looming educational problems, has been thought of with such negative connotations. This does not mean to imply that teachers have not been concerned or have not accomplished remarkable results through intuitive and sensitive teaching. They have understood the child who came late only to fall asleep on his desk; they have seen the overcrowded room where he lives. Lunch programs have been provided; they have seen the food that he eats. They have criticized the stereotyped middle class illustrations of the basal readers. The pictures have been changed so that the child might better identify with the picture. Unfortunately, however, the text continued to be a puzzle. Games have been constructed to motivate and reinforce, but too often the games became an added mystery in that they reinforced what couldn't be understood in the first place. The value of sympathy and interest is not to be questioned— it has just not been enough. Teachers would be the first to admit this as well as the fact that their preservice and in-service preparation seldom provided the help and preparation that they needed. Many excellent courses and workshops have been designed for the purpose of understanding minority groups. These have generally been from the viewpoint of the sociologist and psychologist, however, with little done about the understanding of language and language learning. Just trying new materials designed for standard English is no substitute for understanding the child's dialect. A recent country-wide survey[1] indicates that, within the school districts responding, only 15 percent of the elementary school teachers had had work in this area of teaching English as a second language and only nine percent had practice-taught in the field. In a convention speech of the New Jersey Education Association, Elaine Adler, co-consultant in English as a Second Language on the staff of the New Jersey State Department of Education, appealed to administrators to provide in-service English as a second language training program for their staffs. She continued to say:

> However, in-service training is only one aspect of a teacher training program. Preservice work should be part of the college curriculum of every undergraduate who plans to teach children who do not speak English or a standard dialect of English. Such a curriculum would include courses in linguistics, methods of teaching English as a second language and cultural anthropology.[1]

Communities across the nation have responded to such pleas by publishing handbooks which vary from several pages to extensive lists of materials complete with daily lesson plans. Among these are:

1. El Paso Public Schools, *Teacher's Handbook for Use With Non-English Speaking Pupils* (El Paso, Texas: 1966).
2. Hartford Public Schools, *Hints for Regular Classroom Teachers and*

---

[1] Elaine Adler, Speech given at the Convention of New Jersey Education Association (Atlantic City, New Jersey, November, 1968).

Special Teachers Having Non-English Speaking Pupils (Hartford, Connecticut: 1959).
3. Milwaukee Public Schools, *A Teacher's Guide: Non-English Speaking Pupils* (Milwaukee, Wisconsin: 1963).
4. Texas Education Agency, *Preschool Instructional Program for Non-English Speaking Children* (Austin, Texas: 1964).

Other communities have published readers written for the specific needs of their student population. Examples of these are *The Miami Linguistic Readers* which are Spanish-English based and the *Great Cities Series,* oriented to the problems of the inner city schools of Detroit. Records in Texas, where the problems of Mexican children are statewide, show up to 80 percent of these children repeat first grade. With the aid of a government grant, a highly structured Developmental Oral Language (DOL)[2] program has met with significant success. The school system of St. Louis has preferred to adopt a non-graded primary organization as a means of providing opportunity to strengthen the oral skills for groups that need a longer readiness period. Perhaps two of the most encouraging developments are the summer institutes for teachers under the sponsorship of the National Defense Education Act and the establishment of TESOL, a national professional organization for *Teachers of English to Speakers of Other Languages.* They hold regular meetings, encourage research, publish a journal, and cooperate in programs designed to strengthen the teaching of English.

From the linguistic research in how language is acquired, how language is described, and how it functions, and from such endeavors as those mentioned above, there are some clear-cut messages for all teachers who wish to find direction for language teaching. Their growing interest and concerted efforts may well forecast the possible prevention of failure-oriented situations found in the divergent dialect groups.

To understand the difficulties that a divergent speaker encounters in the regular classroom, it might be effective to pause here and do a little role playing. To do this, imagine that you are a primary grade child and that your dialect is such that
1. There is no phoneme for [T] as heard in *Tom,* but instead you substitute the sound represented by the letter [l]. If this seems too ridiculous an illustration, remember that the German demonstrates a similar difficulty when he says *vind* for *wind.* The [w] simply isn't in

---

[2] Harold B. Allen, *A Survey of the Teaching of English to Non-English Speakers in the United States* (Champaign, Illnois: National Council of Teachers of English, 1966), pp. 28-29.

his stock of phonemes. He can neither say nor hear it just as the American fails to hear or reproduce a good ümlaute.
2. The [u] as heard in *fun* is pronounced as the [a] in *father*. This is understandable, too. Doesn't the Bostonian [a] in *car* sound like the vowel in *yacht*?

Unaware of the fact that you are different, you arrive at your new school. You are to become a reader. The teacher is passing out those beautiful new books that have been used as bait all through the readiness weeks. NOW WE ARE READY!

"Open to the first page," the teacher says gleefully.

You follow the directions carefully. You open the book and behold! A beautiful picture. You caught one of those where you used to live. "A klinkerseck! A klinkerseck!" you shout enthusiastically. The teacher looks at you quickly. The class looks, too. There is silence.

"This is a tadpole. Isn't it children?" She said this very sweetly but firmly. "Now we will read our first lesson. This tadpole's name is *LUN*. Repeat it, children." The class says *LUN*. You say *LAHN*. (Remember your [u]). "This tadpole's name is *TUN*. Repeat it, children." The class says *TUN*. You say LAHN. (Remember your [t]).

Now you must understand that the teacher can't really hear your pronunciation when listening to twenty-two other voices at the same time so she says, "Just fine" to the whole class. In the meantime, you've received good positive reinforcement for the reading of *LUN* as *LAHN* and for *TUN* as *LAHN*. You're even showing the signs of a good reader by asking critical questions like, "Why did both klinkers—I mean tadpoles have the same names?" You're asking it silently this time for the teacher might look at you again. Now you eagerly turn to the next page. Another beautiful picture. Everybody reads with the teacher "Lun and Tun have fun," but you read, "Lahn and Lahn have fahn."

The teacher now turns to the chalkboard and says, "Now we're going to do some rhyming games."

At the word *game* everybody stirs with excitement, including you. The teacher is ready with the question, "Who could tell me where Lun and Tun had fun? Remember it must rhyme,"

You just can't wait. You see the teacher pointing at that glorious sun in the picture but you have your own idea. After all, isn't this a game? "On the lawn," you shout with glee. There's that smile again but the crease on her forehead shows even more. She tries to ignore you. Now she is reinforcing the rhyming lesson with words like *bun, fun,* and *gun*. But because you say, *bahn, fahn* and *gahn,* you are reminded of other words like *gone, dawn,* and *pawn*. If the teacher would only play the homonym twin game, you could offer gun/gone.

The next lesson goes beyond word skills. You're ready for the discussion. First, the teacher is directing the class to read it again. "Lun and Tun had fun in the sun." (Lahn and Lahn had fahn in the sahn.) "Lun splashed Tun." (Lahn splashed Lahn.)

1. What are Lun and Tun doing? Everybody knows they're splashing because you can see it in the picture. "Splashing. Splashing!" they all shout. You enjoy a moment of ecstacy. The teacher smiles and the crease isn't on her forehead this time.
2. What did Lun do? "He splashed." The teacher seems to like you again. Discussions are more fun than word skills.
3. Who did Lun splash? "Lahn splashed Lahn," you answered. The class looked at you again. The teacher looked, too.

You are now grouped with the Cat Fish which are called Bull Heads in your dialect. In the teacher's language, it's the non-reader, the slow learner, and the potential drop-out. Now we must diagnose your difficulty. Perhaps it's low IQ. You may be culturally deprived. You could be immature and need more readiness books with more pictures of Tun and Lun rhyming with *bun* but not with *gone*. Perhaps you need another hearing test? Or an eye test? What do YOU think your trouble was? Certainly, it's not your IQ, and you're surrounded by good books and music and everything cultural in your home. Would more workbook drills with Tun really help? Obviously the language signals of your dialect permit you to read *Tun* as *Lahn*; and these signals have a neuromuscular control over a different set of signals than those used by the teacher and the text. Wouldn't it have helped if the teacher had recognized the specific variations in your dialect and had adjusted her materials and lessons accordingly?

Unfortunately, the illustration you have just considered is not exaggerated. Think of the number of children from Spanish speaking communities who begin to read with *Seep* and *Seep* (Zip and Sip) for example. Their teachers develop consonant substitution lessons based on Zip and Sip. Think of the number of children whose pronunciation patterns demand that such pairs as *beer/bear, bad/bed, pen/pin, oiled/old* and *want/wont* be listed as homonyms and that *Ruth/roof done/dawn* be listed as rhyming words. Can something be done? Yes. A growing group of teachers and school systems across the country are finding agreement in certain basic principles as summarized here.

1. *What goals should be set for students?*
2. *What are the specific syntactic and phonological differences that must be known in order to better understand the learner's language?*
3. *What are the principles of teaching a second dialect?*
4. *What are the methods and materials?*

1. What Goals Should Be Set for Students?

1. To want to learn the standard dialect and to consider it his right rather than an obligation to the teacher and the school.
2. To develop the attitude that a language must be judged in terms of its appropriateness to the situation in which it is used.
3. To acquire a flexibility in language appropriate to a variety of needs and situations.
4. To gain a respect for and an appreciation of linguistic variations which he considers *different* rather than *wrong*.
5. To master the basic sentence and intonation patterns with an ability to expand into a variety of complex sentences.

2. What Are the Specific Syntactical and Phonological Differences that Must Be Known in Order to Better Understand the Learner's Language?

While it is impractical to expect all teachers to be bilingual or even bidialectical, it is not unrealistic to assume that they should know the points at which the learner's language and the target language contrast. With this information they not only can better understand the child when he speaks, but they can make adjustments in the reading and spelling generalizations which ignore language divergencies.

The features described in this section are typical of many groups of non-standard users and can serve as a guide for the development of a list based on the *specific* language patterns found in a particular community. For purposes of space, just two language groups will be analyzed —the black area dialect and the Spanish-American.

Description of Black Area Dialect

The Syntax

1. The Noun and Pronoun.
    a. Plural form. The standard plural form is used but there is a tendency to overextend it in such words as *teeths, mens, sheeps, postes.*
        The plural is not expressed, however, when there is a quantitative word before the noun as in *three cent* or *many boat.*
    b. Possession. The possessive form (*'s*) is dropped when the name of the possessor precedes the name of the thing being possessed.

A phrase such as *The teacher book* relies on juxtaposition and intonation rather than the *'s* to express possession.

The possessive form of the pronoun is built on the pattern of my/mine. This results in such patterns as *ourn/yourn, hisn/hern, ourn/theirn* which produce: *That's hisn. It's yourn. It's theirn.*

   c. The reflective pronoun. They are *theyselves, his self,* producing such patterns as *They used it theyselves. He did it hiself.*
   d. The objective pronoun. This form is also in the nominative producing such patterns as *Me got this. Him gone.*
   e. *You* replaces *your,* producing *You car is smashed.*
   f. *Them* replaces *those,* producing *Them books.*

2. The Article.
   a. The definite article is omitted before nouns. *You knows what crab is? I went to hospital.* When the article is used, however, the *a* form is used in all cases producing: *a* (not *an*) *elephant.*

3. The Adjective.
   a. Comparative and superlative forms. All adjectives are given the form *more* and *most* producing such forms as *more better, most coldest.*

      Note here that a number of these sequences such as the pronoun forms and double comparisons are found in the immature speech patterns of all children. While they disappear in the language of the standard speaker as a normal developmental process, they remain firmly jelled in the patterns of the non-standard speaker.

4. The Verb. This is perhaps the area of greatest difficulty and the learning of the new verb forms is as difficult for them as it would be for the standard speaker to say *He run* instead of *He runs.*
   a. First and third person forms. The *s* is added to the first person singular and third person plural but dropped from the third person singular, presenting such forms as *I walks, He walk, They walks.*
   b. Verbs *do* and *got.* These have special forms, producing *He do* instead of *He does, I does* instead of *I do, He gots* instead of *He got.*
   c. Past tense signals. The forms *t, d, ed* affixed to the verb to form past tense are omitted, producing *I end(ed) up fighting. I wash(ed) my hair.*
   d. The verb *to be.* This verb presents particular difficulty in that it is often dropped both as a linking verb and as an auxiliary. When

it is used, it serves different purposes than those of standard English. Typical omissions produce: *She (is a) good teacher. They (are) here.*

Teachers correcting papers written by these children become confused as they find what seems to be a shifting tense. It is not so much a lack of time concept but rather the way in which time is constructed in their syntax. One teacher evaluating the sequence, *She singing a song,* marked it as a sentence fragment. This time the student was confused.

e. The auxiliary verb. This form is either omitted or replaced by some form of *been.* In this case, it is not interpreted as a tense signal which is the real function of standard English auxiliaries. This produces, *What (are) you fixin' to do? You (are) just so confus(ed). She (will) scold you, tomorrow. He (is) dead already. I (am) tired. I be tired. She bes (is) my best friend.*

f. Future tense. Typical expressions in this form are, *She be scoldin' you. She scold you tomorrow. She goin* (or *gonna*) *scold you.*

5. Sentence Patterns.
   a. The question. The form of *do* and *does* as found in the standard pattern is omitted, producing *How (does) he do that? How (do) them get it?*
   b. *There are* sequences. It is substituted for *there are* and *there is,* producing *It wasn't nobody home. It was nothin' there.*
   c. Negative statements. The word *ain't* substitutes for *hasn't, didn't* as well as for the more general *is not, am not, are not,* producing, *He ain't (hasn't) talk(ed) all day. He ain't gone. He ain't (didn't) learn it. Ain't he come?*

   The negative compounds indefinitely in that the negative quality is attached to every indefinite pronoun or adverb. This results in *Nobody don't have it. I ain't never got no candy from none of them.*

The Phonology

1. The [th] of *thin* becomes *tin.* The [th] of *this* becomes *dis.* The [th] at the end of a word as in *mouth* becomes *mouf* or *mouv.* The [th] in the middle of a word as in *nothing* becomes *nuttin.*

2. The final consonant clusters. These endings are either weakened or dropped producing, *I slamm(ed) the door. I as(ked) good . Mas(k) clas(p).*

Note that because of these omissions, such words as *fin(d) and fine* or *min(d)* and *mine* can be considered homonyms.

3. Initial consonant clusters. These initial groups are given different sounds.

str as in *street* becomes *skreet.*   *shr* as in *shrimp* becomes *shwimp.*
tr as in *tree* becomes *chree.*   *dr* as in *drum* becomes *trum.*

4. Short vowel sounds. Words distinguished by the short vowel in the standard dialect do not have these distinctions in the pronounciation of the nonstandard. This produces such contrasts as: *He be ol(d); The car ol(d)* (oiled); *That be ol(d)* (all) for standard *old, oiled, all. I been slam da dough* (door) for the standard *dough* and *door. It make a big far* for the standard *fire* and *far. She use no pen* for the standard *pen* and *pin. He wont* (wants) *lunch* for the standard *want, wont.*

5. -*ing* verb ending. This sound at the end of verbs is either omitted or shortened to *in.* This procedure, *Good mornin* or *Good morn* with an elongated *n.*

6. The [r]. This sound is dropped making the *r* controlled rule unrealistic.

Description of Spanish Language Forms

While there are many publications designed for the teaching of English to children from Spanish speaking homes, these materials are more generally available to the language specialists who reach a limited number of children in the elementary school. Extending these programs alone cannot solve the reading and language problems unless the classroom teacher who works with the children the greatest part of the day has some understanding of the language.

The teacher who may not be bilingual should not minimize the contribution she can make as a native speaker of English who can present a good standard model for the child to imitate.

The Syntax

1. The Noun.
   a. Since possession in Spanish is expressed by the genitive case, the English possessive form is strange. Help is needed in transferring from the *book of the boy* to *the boy's book.*

2. The Pronoun.
   a. Since the subject pronoun is part of the Spanish verb, there is a tendency to omit it. *It is round* becomes *Is round.*
   b. The objective form of the pronoun is used before the verb in the subject position. *Her I know. Him I gave the lesson.*
   c. The relative pronouns (that, who) refer to objects as well as to people. *Carlos is the boy who/that won. That is the movie who/that she saw.*

3. The Verb.
   a. The third person singular form of the verb does not add the *s* ending. *The girl run. The teacher laugh.*
   b. The verb *to have* is used in place of the *to be. I have thirst* (I am thirsty). *I have more years* (I am older).
   c. There is also a tendency to drop the *to be* verb in such sequences as *He doctor* (He is a doctor); *He smart* (He is smart).
   d. There is no auxiliary equivalent to *do, does, did: Where work your father?* (Where does your father work?)
   e. There is no equivalent to the auxiliary *will: The boy study.* (The boy will study.)
   f. There is no equivalent in the future tense for *is, am, are* with the *ing* form: *I go to study.* (I am going to study.)

      Note, then, the ambiguity of the above statement. The intent of the English structured sentence was to state that speaker would study in the future. The Spanish form expresses the reason for going.

4. The Adjective.
   a. The English *-er* and *-est* for comparative forms are not used at all but instead *more* and *most* are placed before all adjectives. *The boy is more big than girl.*
   b. The definite article is used before a title: *The Mr. Bangs is principal. Give it to the Dr. Brown.*
   c. The indefinite article is not used for identification: *He (is) (a) professor. The Miss Smith (is) (a) teacher.*

5. The Preposition.
   a. *In on, at* are used interchangeably: *The letter (is) in the book; . . . on the book; . . . at the book.*

6. Word Order.
   a. The adjective usually follows the noun that it modifies: *The dog big jump.* (The big dog jumps.)

b. The question is signalled by rising pitch and not necessarily by inversion.

c. *No* is placed before the verb to express a command: *No push.*

7. Intonation.   There is a natural tendency to carry over the intonation of the native language to the target language. The small structure words—articles, prepositions, conjunctions and auxiliaries—receive stress and are not slurred over as they are in English. Spanish could be described as a syllable rather than a phrase language.

The Phonology

1. The Vowels.   The very simplicity of the Spanish vowel system presents havoc when translated into the intricate vowel system of English. *First,* the Spanish speaking child who has already learned his alphabet will pronounce the vowels as [ah] [ey] [ee] [ō] [ōō], not as [ā] [ē] [ī] [ō] [ū].

The five vowel phonemes are reflected in the names of the vowels as given above.

[ah]	as in *father*	represented by the letter *a.*
[ey]	as in *they*	represented by the letter *e.*
[ee]	as in *meet*	represented by the letter *i.*
[O]	as in *Oh*	represented by the letter *o.*
[oo]	as in *tool*	represented by the letter *u.*

Second, the child can hear only these five vowel sounds and thus has a difficult time distinguishing between *I have a cut; I have a cot;* and *I have a cat.*

Third, all vowels are pronounced, allowing no opportunity for one vowel to go walking while the other does the talking. Words like *boat* would then become a two-syllable word—*bo-at.* This obviously becomes a language hazard when the syllabication aids to English pronunciations are imposed.

2. The Consonants.   While consonants do not present as great a problem as do the vowels, there are some points of phonological differences that can create serious learning problems. Only those consonants that present the greatest problem will be described here.

a. The *c* has the same description as given in English.

b becomes *p: cab* becomes *cap; rabbit* becomes *rapid*

v becomes *b: vest* becomes *best; five* becomes *fibe*

b. Because of the different tongue positions in Spanish for producing [d] and [t], these sounds can become confused, resulting in *den* for *ten,* and *dis* and *dat* for *this* and *that.*

c. When *g* is followed by *e* or *i* it becomes *h*, but is strongly aspirated like the German *buch,* and *general* becomes *heneral.* It retains the English hard [g] when it precedes a *u* as in *guitar.*

d. While the *q* elicits the [h], the letter *h* elicits silence. *hospital* becomes *ospital, hotel* becomes *otel.*

e. While the letter *l* elicits the same sound as that in English, the *ll* is pronounced like [y] in *yes: llama* becomes *yama.*

f. The *s* receives both the [s] and [z] sounds found in English. When a word starts with an *s*, the Spanish speaking student will automatically place an *e* in front: *student* becomes *estudent.*

g. The *ch* is pronounced like *sh* so that *chew* becomes *shoe; chin* becomes *shin.*

There are several sounds unique to Cuban Spanish which should be considered. The *s* as well as the *h* is silent. *English* becomes *Engli. Sh* becomes *ch; shirt* becomes *chirt.* The consonant clusters will be approximated with the closest sound of his native language so that a great deal of help is required in this area.

The teacher who occasionally uses expressions in the child's native tongue extends a feeling of comfort and security. Too, English-speaking members of the class would benefit and enjoy learning these expressions. A selected list follows:

adiós	goodbye	hoy	today
buenos días	good morning	mañana	tomorrow
hasta mañana	see you tomorrow	magnífico	wonderful
¡Hola!	hi, hello	ahora	now
correcto	OK	fácil	easy
gracias	thank you	¿Cómo te va?	How are you?
		¡Que lástima!	What a shame!
la Pascua	Easter or Christmas	Feliz Navidad or Felices Pascuas	Merry Christmas
El Día de las Madres	Mothers' Day	el árbol de Navidad	Christmas tree
La Vispera de Todos los Santos	Halloween	el hombre de nieve	snowman
la calabaza	pumpkin	el juguete	toy
el gato negro	black cat	San Nicolás	Saint Nicholas—Santa Claus

la máscara	mask	la tarjeta de Navidad	Christmas card
El Día de Gracias	Thanksgiving	Feliz cumpleaños	Happy Birthday
el maíz	corn	Felicidades ati	Happy Birthday to you
el pavo	turkey	Felicidades, (Carmela)	Happy Birthday, (Carmela)
		Felicidades, ati	Happy Birthday to you

3. What Are the Principles of Teaching a Second Dialect?

1. Language is learned through the establishment of automatic neural muscular responses rather than by learning the grammatical rules.

2. The points of difference or contrast must be indicated in the two languages; that is, between the divergent language (or dialect) and the target language, standard English.

3. Exercises should start with the student's form which is then contrasted with the target form. Drill is then placed on the target form, *not to replace* the student form but to serve as *another language or dialect.*

4. Exercises should be interesting, using names of the students and common experiences in preference to already prepared commercial drills.

5. Each lesson should start with a review of known patterns to assure each student of his progress. The use of puppets or dramatic situations gives sprightliness and realistic intonation patterns to what otherwise might be boring and monotonous.

6. The new forms should be learned by analogy and imitation but not by grammatical analysis.

4. What Are the Appropriate Methods and Materials?

This section is divided into two parts: *Part A* describes methods and materials designed to develop a positive attitude toward differences in language. *Part B* presents methods and materials designed to develop proficiency in the use of standard language forms. The section is meant to be a guide for teachers as they construct their own materials appropriate to the needs of a particular class.

Part A   Developing a Positive Attitude toward Differences

Purposes: 1. To develop the principle that the word *dialect* is a label for a variety of speech patterns within a larger language community. As such, it is not a derogatory term.   2. To develop an attitude of acceptance and interest in these differences.

1. Identify well-known entertainers who represent different dialects found in the United States. The most available materials would be found on television and recordings. Discuss their style in terms of specific differences in syntax, pronunciation and vocabulary. Elicit the ideas that:
   a. They are different but not wrong.
   b. They must also know the standard dialect and sometimes several dialects if their parts require it.
   c. There is an advantage in knowing several dialects.

2. Write a sequence according to the dialects of well known actors or actresses. What would you have to do in the writing to show these differences? Do the same using the dialect of a well known comic strip character.

3. Rewrite a comic strip sequence to reflect the speech of "the formal language community."

4. Collect comic strip sequences based on dialect differences. Elicit: Our language is part of our way of life just as much as our actions or what we wear. We can change our clothes; why shouldn't we change the language, too?

5. Listen for dialect differences in TV commercials. Even the youngest children can imitate them. Elicit: I can talk like many people. These sequences can be taped to be readily available in the classroom. Children then make their own sequences and listen to both.

6. Locate poems and stories written in dialect.

7. Develop a chart showing at least three different language patterns: a non-standard form in the student's dialect, the standard form, and the non-standard form of another dialect. The inclusion of the non-standard form places emphasis on the comparison of dialects in

general rather than on the comparison of the student's form to the standard.

While the attitude toward language that has just been proposed is important, to stop there would be to avoid the school's responsibility to provide the opportunity and *right* of every child to gain facility in the standard dialect. These children will succeed better when materials are systematically presented in interesting and varied ways until they gain automatic responses in the standard forms.

Part B   Developing Proficiency in the Use of Standard Language Forms

Using Language Drills: An endless variety of language pattern drills can be constructed by taking the following steps.   1. Refer to the section on the phonological and syntactical differences to determine the point of contrast to be taught.   2. Describe the difference in terms of the muscles that are used to produce the target sound. Compare it to the contrast point in their dialect by slipping from one to the other.   3. Construct frames but elicit content words from the children. Use names and ideas from the environment.

Following are examples of possible constructions.

1. Contrast in noun-verb agreement (Both black and Spanish): *Maria talk fast* to *Maria talks fast*. Note: This agreement is the crux of the English sentence. The misuse of these forms can affect comprehension. While the target form is a declarative sentence simply stating what Mary does, the divergent form, when given the proper intonation (signaled by a comma), could mean that Maria was being told to talk fast, e.g., *Maria, talk fast*. Habit-producing exercises can be constructed by substitution.
   a. Substitute class names for Maria: *Joseph* talks, *Timothy* talks, etc.
   b. Substitute verbs suggested by the children: Joseph *sings,* etc.
   c. Substitute the pronoun for the noun. This is difficult because of the divergent speakers tendency to use the objective pronoun in nominative position: *He* sings, *They* sing, *She* sings.

2. Contrast in the past tense of regular verbs (Both black and Spanish): *He walk* to *He walked*. Feel the sound [d] produced by the tongue on the gum in back of the upper teeth in contrast to the sound [k] produced in the throat.

   To vary the drill, add a prepositional phrase as: *He walked into our room*. In developing this exercise, note that the sequence that follows the verb should start with a vowel because the final sound of the verb is easier to say and to hear when followed by an open vowel than when followed by a closed consonant. For example: *walked in* instead of *walked to.*

3. Contrast in possessive form (Both black and Spanish): *This Marty coat* to *This Marty's coat* to *This is Marty's coat.*
Substitute class names for *Marty.* When this is flowing, substitute other nouns for *coat.* Avoid words that start with [s] because the possessive [s] and the noun phoneme [s] would blend in natural speech.
    Vary the drill by using such question and answer sequences as:
Teacher   Whose coat is this?
Students   This is *Marty's coat* (*Maria's coat, Joseph's coat,* etc.).

4. Construct dialogue frames with content words elicited from the children.
Who sat here?   (Valerie sat here.)
Who sits here?   (Valerie sits here) for (sit here)
Does Nick sit here?   (No, Jose, sits here or No, he sits *here*) for (no sit)
Where are the students?   (They are here or They're here) for (thems here)
Whose book is this?   (It's mine) for (it be mines)
What are you doing?   (I am walking, singing etc.) for (I be walkin)
Who is talking?   (Mary is talking) for (Mary bes talkin)
Did you see the book?   (No, I did not see the book but I saw the _____.)
Does Violet like school?   (No, Violet does not like school; she likes _____.)
    In sequences like those above, do not present the contracted form before the full standard form is understood; for example, *They are here* before *They're here.*

Using Music and Games: Music and games present a natural setting for practice. Suggestions follow but the possibilities are endless.

1. *The Farmer in the Dell:* Alert to *farmer takes* instead of *farmer take.* Watch for front teeth position for [s]. Alert to *the deery oh* instead of *da derry oh.*

2. *Go in and out the window:* Alert to concept of *in* and *out; as you have done before* for *you be done; stand and greet* for *stands and greets.*

3. *London Bridge is Falling Down: Bridge is falling* for *Bridge falling; here come the choppers* for *comes the choppers.*

4. *Did you Ever See a Lassie? See a lassie* for *sees a lassie.*

5. *Here we go Looby Loo: Here we go* for *here we goes; put my right foot* for *I puts my;* concept of right and left.

6. *The Gingerbread Boy: He ran* for *he runned; catch* for *ketch.*

7. *Eensy Weensy Spider:* past tense verbs and concept of direction.

8. *A Goblin Lives in Our House: our* for *ourn;* agreement of subject and verb in the repetitive choruses.
   Build on verses like these by asking questions like, What did all the goblins do? The answer must evoke the plural form of the pronoun and the change of the verb form.
   It would be a mistake to confine the above materials to young children. Most effective programs have been given by upper graders who have expressed these verses and songs through shadow graphs, choral speech, dramatizations etc. *Eensy Weensy Spider* and *There Was a Little Turtle* have all the ingredients for modern dance and original music. These children have ability in this medium. Use it.

9. Dramatizing single phonemes:
   a. zzz as in zebra   A bee or jet zooming through the air. Direct some children to act out the jet or bee while others produce the sound. Test vibration in throat made by [z] and not by [s]. Direct to make sound softer or louder as the objects zoom far away or close by.
   b. [k]   gargling mouthwash
   c. [t] [p]   tip tap: Rain drops? A bird pecking at a tree? A lady walking in high heels?

10. Hearing syllables: (Especially helpful for Spanish children; black children sometimes clap words such as *red* as two syllables because of the glide they give to the phoneme [e]) Let each child decide on the number of claps he hears in his name. He claps while class listens and then he leads class as they clap his name. After the first child's name is clapped, ask all children who have the same number of claps in the name to stand. Test these. Proceed to names with other groups

of syllables and finally arrange in categories. Later help them hear differences in accent in names that have the same number of syllables. For example: [*Val* e rie] and [Ma *Ri* a].

For variation bounce a large and small ball. Proceed to words after names are mastered.

Suggestions for Further Study

1. Find examples of verses that rhyme when pronounced according to standard dialect but would not rhyme if read according to the sound patterns described in this chapter.

2. Discuss how the weakened or omitted consonants on the end of words affect comprehension; for example: a. delay(ed) green light—to delay the light or the light is delayed? b. crush(ed) ice—crush the ice or the ice is crushed?

3. Examine the Linguistic Atlas. What explanations do you find for variations in American English?

4. React to the following: Language in America experienced changes caused by the Industrial Revolution and the development of the railroads. For this reason, the typical unit on communication which stresses inventions only should be expanded to facts about language and how and why it changed.

5. What is the difference between unacceptable usage patterns and the regional dialect of educated persons?

6. Write a sequence in which a salesman is trying to sell you a new car. Revise it using non-standard forms. Which version would be most effective in persuading you to buy? Discuss in terms of the principle of appropriate speech and job mobility.

7. Make a collection of "Usage lessons" as presented in many textbooks. React to them in terms of what you know about how language is learned or changed. React in terms of what you know about levels of speech and language change.

8. The house rules listed in a hotel on the Island of Maui read as follows:
   You must pay you rent in advance.
   You must not let you room go one day back.
   Women are not allow in you room.

You are not allow to gamble in you room.
Only on Sunday you can sleep all day.
You are not allow in the dinering room or in the seating room when you drunk.
If you can't keep this rules please don't take the room.
What syntactical forms seem to be causing difficulty? What would you do if you were to teach in Hawaii?

9. The principal parts of the verb of certain mountain speech are:

ax (ask)	axt	axt
bring	brung	brung
sneak	snuk	snuk

If you were to teach in the Ozarks, how would you adjust your English lessons?

10. Consider the following sequences from the Pennsylvania Dutch Country in the same way that you considered exercises 8 and 9 above.

Late it be already.   Make the door shut.
It's some warm today.   Let's walk the road down.
Throw the cow over the fence some hay.

11. The following sequences are taken from the *Dictionary of the Underworld**: You're all caught up (marked for death). No more contracts (favors). I'm rip (aware) you were spending all the swag (stolen goods). Are there other dictionaries devoted to the vocabulary of special groups? Share some of your findings. Write a dictionary of words special to the teaching profession or to any special group you choose. Discuss this assignment in terms of the statement, "Language reflects the culture."

Useful References for Second Language Teaching

I.   Professional Organizations

Center for Applied Linguistics: A coordinating body for linguistic studies. Issues a newsletter, *The Linguistuc Reporter,* six times per year. Annual subscription, $1.50. Center for Applied Linguistics, 1717 Massachusetts Avenue, N.W., Washingon, D.C. 20036.

---

* Eric Partridge, *Dictionary of the Underworld,* rev. ed. (New York: The Macmillan Company, 1961).

National Association for Foreign Student Affairs (NAFSA). Publishes NAFSA newsletter. United Nations Plaza, New York.

National Council of Teachers of English. Professional journals include *Elementary English, English Journal,* and *College English* as well as many publications in this field. Champaign, Ill.

Teachers of English to Speakers of Other Languages (TESOL). There are branches in many states. Publishes *TESOL Newsletter* and *TESOL Quarterly.* Membership, $10.00. Executive Secretary of TESOL, School of Languages and Linguistics, Georgetown University, Washington, D.C. 20007.

II.   Booklists and Materials

Aaron, A., ed. *TESOL Bibliography.* Miami, Fla.: *Florida FL Reporter,* 1967.

Byron Book Co. *Ethnic Bibliography.* 3 issue 2, West Lynn, Oregon, 97068.

Center for Applied Linguistics. *English as a Second Language in the Elementary Schools: Background and Text Materials.* Washington, D.C. 1966.

Children's Music Center. *Ingles Para Ninos,* Los Angeles: Los Angeles Music Center.

One LP record with illustrated book presenting English to Spanish-speaking children.

Council on Interracial Books for Children, Inc. *Quarterly Newsletter.* New York.

Crowell, Collier & Macmillan, Inc. *Catalog: The Collier-Macmillan English Program.* 1971. 866 Third Ave., New York, 10022.

Lists a variety of graded materials including *English 900,* self-instructional materials, books based on specialized professions.

Educational Reading Service. *Stepping Stones.* Mahwah, N.J.: Educational Reading Service, 1969.

A catalog of multi-racial and multi-ethnic learning materials about Negro, Puerto Rican, Mexican-American, American Indian and other children. Records, filmstrips, books and transparencies.

Hopkins, Lee B. *Let Them Be Themselves.* New York: Citation Press, 1969.

Appendix contains a booklist entitled *The Urban and Disadvantaged Child.*

International Film Bureau. *A Foreign Language.* Washington, D.C.

A filmed classroom demonstration of methods which help children of different language backgrounds speak English.

National Council of Teachers of English, Chalemae Rollins, ed. *We Build Together—A Reader's Guide to Negro Life and Literature for Elementary and High School Use.* Champaign, Ill., 1968.

Pan American Union. *Proyecto Leer Bulletin.* Bulletin 6. Washington, D.C. Summer, 1969.

Scholastic Magazines. *Foreign Language Periodicals.* Englewood Cliffs, N.J.

Offers student subscriptions to ten periodicals published in French, Spanish, German or Russian. Companion record sets are also available. Their publication *Scope* offers high interest materials with low readability levels.

Schotta, Sarita G. *Teaching English as a Second Language.* Davis, Calif.: University of California Press, Spring, 1966.

Wheeler, Gonzales. *Exchanging Greetings and Introductions.* New York: McGraw-Hill Book Co., 1969.

An excellent aid for demonstration and practice. Part of the *Let's Speak English* series designed for use from kindergarten through sixth grade. The International Division of this company offers a catalogue of a wide variety of materials for second language teaching.

III.   Children's Books in the Spanish Language*

Elkin, Benjamin. *El hombre que camino alrededor del mundo.* Chicago: Children's Press, Inc., 1961.

An old tale about a wild goose chase involving a lucky Boola bird.

Ets, Marie Hall. *Gilberto y el viento.* New York: The Viking Press, Inc., 1967.

A small boy plays with his unpredictable friend, the wind.

Leaf, Munro, *El cuento de Ferdinando.* New York: The Viking Press, Inc., 1962.

Ferdinand, probably the only bull who prefers flowers to fighting.

Lenski, Lois. *El auto pequeno.* New York: Henry Z. Walck, Inc., 1968.

The story of Mr. Small and his little red automobile is a classic delight.

---

* These books are also printed in English.

Politi, Leo. *Pedro el angel de la Calle Olvera*. New York: Charles Scribner's Sons, 1961.

Pedro, who sings like an angel, is chosen to lead La Posada, a traditional Christmas ceremony in the Mexican section of Los Angeles.

Politi, Leo. *Rosa*. New York: Charles Scribner's Sons, 1963.

Longing for a doll of her own, Rosa is overjoyed to find a real live baby in her home.

Rey, Hans A. *Jorge el curioso*. Boston: Houghton Mifflin Co., 1961.

The city adventures of Curious George, the monkey.

(See catalogues for Follett Educational Corporation, McGraw-Hill, Inc., and Educational Reading Service as well as those textbook companies listed. The Buffalo and Erie County Public Library, Buffalo, N.Y., issues an excellent annotated book list printed in Spanish and English.)

IV.   Books to Help Bridge the Understanding Gap

Bontemps, Anna, ed. *Golden Slippers: An Anthology of Negro Poetry*. New York: Harper & Row, Publishers, 1941.

Cavanna, Betty. *Carlos of Mexico*. New York: Franklin Watts, Inc., 1964.

Clayton, Edward T. *Martin Luther King: The Peaceful Warrior*. New York: Prentice-Hall, Inc., 1964.

Cohen, Robert. *The Color of Man*. New York: Random House, Inc., 1968.

Colorado, Antonio. *The First Book of Puerto Rico*. New York: Franklin Watts, Inc., 1965.

Epstein, Samuel. *The First Book of Mexico*, rev. ed. New York: Franklin Watts, Inc., 1967.

Geis, Darlene. *Let's Travel in Mexico*. Chicago: Children's Press, Inc., 1961.

Hughes, Langston. *First Book of Jazz*. New York: Franklin Watts, Inc., 1954.

Keats, Ezra Jack. *The Snowy Day*. New York: The Viking Press, Inc., 1962; *Whistle for Willie*. New York: The Viking Press, Inc., 1964.

Both these books are published in sound-filmstrips by Weston Woods, Inc., Weston Woods, Conn.

Larralde, Elsa. *The Land and People of Mexico*. Philadelphia: J. B. Lippincott Co., 1964.

Lerner, Marguerite Rush. *Red Man, White Man, African Chief: The Story of Skin Color*. New York: Lerner Publications Co., 1960.

McGuire, Edna. *Puerto Rico: Bridge to Freedom.* New York: The Macmillan Co., 1963.

Robinson, Donald W. *As Others See Us.* Boston, Houghton-Mifflin, 1969.

Robinson, Ray. *The Greatest World Series Thrillers.* New York: Random House, Inc., 1965.

Senior, Clarence O. *The Puerto Ricans: Strangers–Then Neighbors.* New York: Quadrangle Books, Inc., 1965.

V.   Counting, Rhyming and Rhythms

Educational Reading Service. *Paso a Paso.* Mahwah, N.J., 1967.

Long-play recording of rhymes and games. Spanish–English notes.

Mother Goose. *Mother Goose in Spanish.* New York: Thomas Y. Crowell Co., 1968.

Resnick, Seymour. *Selections from Spanish Poetry.* Irvington on the Hudson, N.Y.: Harvey House, Inc., Publishers, 1962.

Stanek, Muriel N. *One, Two, Three for Fun.* Chicago: Albert Whitman & Co., 1967.

General Bibliography

Books

Aarons, Alfred C., et al., ed. *Linguistic-Cultural Differences and American Education.* Vol. 7, No. 1, Miami, Fla.: *The Florida Fl Reporter* (Spring, 1969).

Allen, Harold, ed. *Readings in Applied English Linguistics.* New York: Appleton-Century-Crofts, 1958 (paperback).

Not recent but still a good collection of articles about language.

Allen, Harold. *Teaching English as a Second Language.* New York: Mc-Graw-Hill Book Co., 1965.

A basic book for this area of study. Good analysis of languages and dialects with section on testing second language learning.

Bruner, Jerome S. *The Process of Education.* Cambridge, Mass.: Harvard University Press, 1962.

The principles presented apply to linguistic methodology.

Carroll, John B. *The Study of Language.* Cambridge, Mass.: Harvard University Press, 1953.

Cazden, Courtney B. *Language in Early Childhood and Reading: A Review for 1969/70.* Washington, D.C.: Center for Applied Linguistics, 1970.

Dechant, Emerald, *Linguistics, Phonics and the Teaching of Reading.* Springfield, Ill.: Charles C. Thomas, Publisher, 1969.

Eldonna, Everetts, ed. *Dimensions of Dialect.* Champaign, Ill.: N.C.T.E., 1967.

Finocchiaro, Mary. *Teaching English as a Second Language,* rev. ed. New York: Harper & Row, Publishers, 1969.

Francis, Nelson. *The Structure of American English.* New York: The Ronald Press Co., 1958.

The last chapter is devoted to the teaching aspect; contains good section on American English dialects.

Fries, Charles C. *The Structure of English.* New York: Harcourt, Brace & World, Inc., 1952.

Good introduction to the construction of English sentences.

————. *Linguistics and Reading.* New York: Holt, Rinehart & Winston, Inc., 1952.

Offers a presentation of word patterns and the theory of the "transfer stage" to reading.

Hanna, Paul, et al. *Spelling Structures and Strategies.* Boston: Houghton Mifflin Co., 1971.

Thorough and readable presentation of grapheme-phoneme relationships and their significance in the teaching of word skills.

Hunt, Kellog W. *Differences in Grammatical Structures—Written at Three Grade Levels.* Cooperative Research Project #1998, Office of Health, Education and Welfare, 1964, N.C.T.E. Research Report #3.

Good guide to curriculum building and language evaluation.

Joos, Martin. *The Five Clocks of English Usage.* New York: Harcourt, Brace & World, Inc., 1967.

Highly interesting presentation of levels of usage and theory of language flexibility and appropriateness.

Lefevre, Carl A. *Linguistics and the Teaching of Reading.* New York: McGraw-Hill Book Co., 1964.

Emphasizes power of intonation in reading comprehension.

————. *Linguistics, English, and the Language Arts.* Boston: Allyn & Bacon, Inc., 1970.

Loban, Walter D. *The Language of Elementary School Children.* Champaign, Ill.: N.C.T.E. Research Report #1, 1963.

Research findings of syntactical patterns found in children's language.

McDavid, Raven I., Jr. *American Social Dialects.* Champaign, Ill.: N.C.T.E., 1955.

Malstom, Jean and Ashley, Annabel. *Dialects, U.S.A.* Champaign, Ill.: N.C.T.E., 1967.

Contains good material for teacher preparing a unit.

Partridge, Eric. *Dictionary of the Underworld,* rev. ed. New York: The Macmillan Co., 1961.

Presents fascinating insights into language. See, too, his other dictionaries of Cliches and of Unconventional English.

Pooley, Robert C. *Teaching English Usage.* New York: Appleton-Century-Crofts, 1946.

Old but still a popular reference. Good section on what and what not to teach.

Roberts, Paul. *Patterns of English.* New York: Harcourt, Brace & World, Inc., 1956.

Well developed and sometimes amusing descriptions of English syntax. Good supplement to Fries' books listed above.

Riessman, Frank. *Helping the Disadvantaged Pupil to Learn More Easily.* Englewood, N.J.: Prentice-Hall, Inc., 1966.

Shuy, Roger and Baratz, Joan C. ed. *Teaching Black Children to Read.* Washington, D.C.: Center for Applied Linguistics, 1969.

Considers the importance of experiential background and dialect in the process of reading.

Smith, Frank. *Understanding Reading.* New York: Holt, Rinehart & Winston, Inc., 1971.

A psycholinguistic analysis of the reading process. Original and fresh approach.

Stewart, William A., ed. *Non-Standard Speech and the Teaching of English.* Washington, D.C.: Center for Applied Linguistics, 1964.

Offers insight into study of a still controversial subject.

Strickland, Ruth C. *The Construction of Structural Linguistics to the Teaching of Reading, Writing and Grammar in the Elementary School.* Bulletin of the School of Education, Bloomington, Ind., Indiana University, 1964.

Westmore, Thomas H., ed. *Linguistics in the Classroom.* Champaign, Ill.: N.C.T.E., 1963.

Eight articles reprinted from the *English Journal.* Classroom point of view.

Professional Journals and Yearbooks

Albright, R. W. and Albright, J. B. "Application of Descriptive Linguistics to Child Language." *Journal of Speech Research* 1 (1958) 257–61.

Allen, Robert L. "Better Reading Through the Recognition of Grammatical Relations." *The Reading Teacher* 18 (December, 1964) 194–98.

Bailey, Beryl L. "Toward a New Perspective in Negro English Dialectology." *American Speech* 40 (October, 1965) 171–77.

_____. "Some Aspects of the Impact of Linguistics on Language Teaching in Disadvantaged Communities." *Elementary English* 45 (May, 1968) 570–78, 626.

Blimenfeld, Jacob and Miller, Gerlad. "Improving Reading Through Grammatical Constraints." *Elementary English* 43 (November, 1966) 752–55.

Bordie, John G. "When Should Instruction in a Second Language or Dialect Begin?" *Elementary English* 48 (May, 1971) 551–54.

Brown, Roger and Bellugi, Ursula. "Three Processes in the Child's Acquisition of Syntax." *Harvard Educational Review* 34 (Spring, 1964) 133–51.

Card, William and McDavid, Virginia. "Frequencies of Structure Words in the Writing of Children and Adults." *Elementary English* 42 (December, 1965) 878–82.

Davis, Allison. "Teaching Reading and Language to Disadvantaged Negro Children." *Elementary English* 42 (November, 1965) 791–97.

Ervin, Susan and Miller, Wick R. "Language Development." Edited by H. W. Stevenson, *Sixty-Second Yearbook*, Part I. National Society for the Study of Education, Chicago: University of Chicago Press, 1963, pp. 108–43.

Goodman, Kenneth. "A Communicative Theory of the English Curriculum." *Elementary English* 40 (March, 1963) 290–98.

————. "Dialect Barriers to Reading Comprehension." *Elementary English* 42 (December, 1965) 854–60.

————. "Word Perception: Linguistic Bases." *Education* 87 (May, 1967) 539–43.

Hunt, Kellog W. "Recent Measures in Syntactic Development." *Elementary English* 43 November, 1966) 732–39.

International Reading Association. *The Reading Teacher*. 18 (December, 1964).

Jensen, J. Vernon. "Effects of Childhood Bilingualism." *Elementary English* 39 (April, 1962) 132–43.

Johnson, Kenneth R. "Teacher's Attitude Toward the Nonstandard Negro Dialect." *Elementary English* 48 (February, 1971) 176–82.

Keyser, Samuel Jay. "The Role of Linguistics in the Elementary School Curriculum." *Elementary English* 47 (January, 1970) 39–45.

Kirton, Carole Masley. "Language Acquisition and Development: Some Implications for the Classroom." *Elementary English* 48 (March, 1971) 406–12.

Lefevre, Carl A. "Reading Instruction Related to Primary Language Learning: A Linguistic View." *Journal of Developmental Reading* 4 (Spring, 1961) 147–58.

————. "A Comprehensive Linguistic Approach to Reading." *Elementary English* 42 (October, 1965) 651–59.

Lloyd, Donald. "Intonation and Reading." *Education* 84 (May, 1964) 533–41.

————. "Structure in Language." *College English* 24 (November, 1964) 598–602.

McNeill, David. "The Capacity for Language Acquisition." *The Volta Review* 68 (January, 1966) 17–32.

Marquardt, William F. "Language Interference in Reading." *The Reading Teacher* 18 (December, 1964) 214–18.

Menyuk, Paul. "The Syntactic Rules Used by Children from Preschool through First Grade." *Child Development* 35 (1964) 533–46.

Pertz, Doris L. "Urban Youth, Nonstandard English & Economic Mobility." *Elementary English* 48 (December, 1971) 1012–16.

Ponder, Eddie G. "Understanding the Language of the Culturally Disadvantaged Child." *Elementary English* 42 (November, 1965) 769–74.

Rojas, Pauline M. "Reading Materials for Bilingual Children." *Elementary School Journal* 47 (December, 1946) 204–11.

Sabaroff, Rose E. "Improving Achievement in Beginning Reading: A Linguistic Approach." *The Reading Teacher* 23 (March, 1970) 523–27.

Smith, Dora V. "Growth in Language Power as Related to Child Development." *Teaching Language in the Elementary School, Forty-Third Yearbook*, Part II. The National Society for the Study of Education, Chicago: University of Chicago Press, 1964, 52–97.

Stevens, Martin. "Intonation and the Teaching of Reading." *Elementary English* 42 (March, 1965) 231–37.

Venezky, Richard L. "Reading: Grapheme-Phoneme Relationship." *Education* 87 (May, 1967) 519–24.

Wardhaugh, Ronald. "A Linguist Looks at Phonics." *Elementary English* 48 (January, 1971) 61–67.

Wilson, Rosemary. "Applying Linguistics to Remedial Reading." *The Reading Teacher* 16 (May, 1963) 452–55.

Wilt, Miriam. "Talk-Talk-Talk." *The Reading Teacher* 21 (April, 1968) 611–18.

Yandall, Maurine and Zintz, Milea U. "Some Difficulties Which Indian Children Encounter with Idioms in Reading." *Reading Teacher* 14 (March, 1961) 256–59.